THE LITTLE BOOK
OF THE
ICELANDERS
IN THE OLD DAYS

ALDA SIGMUNDSDÓTTIR

THE LITTLE BOOK
OF THE
ICELANDERS
IN THE OLD DAYS

ENSKA TEXTASMIÐJAN

TABLE OF CONTENTS

A brief historical timeline of Iceland. 7

Introduction. 9

1 Turf. 13

2 Bath parlour. 15

3 Stayin' awake. 18

4 Read on. 20

5 Pecking order. 22

6 Waking sticks. 26

7 Let there be light. 29

8 Ceremony of light-time. 32

9 Let there be daylight. 33

10 The high risk of pregnancy. 36

11 A child makes it into the world!. 40

12 Naming jinx. 42

13 Battle over the young soul. 43

14 A brief lecture about elves. 45

15 Those crafty hidden folk and their opulent lives. . . . 48

16 Mountain dairy. 50

17 Spring. 54

18 Making hay. 56

19 And of course, those ubiquitous superstitions. 58

20 Kiddie workers. 60

21 Whipped into love. 62

22 The farmers who rowed. 65

23 Foremen's intuition. 67

24 Seafaring superstitions. 69

25 Bounty. 72

26 Indebted to the district. 76

27 Lamb in a barrel. 79

28 What the sheep gave. 81

29 Leadership. I mean sheep. 83

30 Food glorious food. .85

31 Ration. 87

32 Grains and subs. 90

33 The absent food group. 92

34 Annihilation of the pearly whites. 94

35 Precious salt. 96

36 Beggars and vagabonds. 97

37 Aliens in Iceland. .101

38 A visitor comes to the farm. 103

39 Godding on the window. 106

40 Come happy, go happy, eat happy. 108

41 Offensive sex. 111

42 Blue verses. 113

43 Fun fun fun. 115

44 Going to town. 119

45 Grunge scene. 121

46 Grim reaper. 125

47 Grief box. 127

48 Death superstitions. 128

49 Last rites. 131

50 The role of hope. .134

In closing. 138

Acknowledgements. 138

A very special thank you. 139

About the author. 140

Sources 141

A BRIEF HISTORICAL TIMELINE OF ICELAND

873-930 Settlement

930 Alþingi, Iceland's parliament, is established at Þingvellir

1000 Christianity is imposed

1262-1264 Iceland comes under Norwegian rule

1262 The Little Ice Age begins

1380 Iceland becomes part of the Kalmar Union

1550 The Reformation. Lutheranism is imposed.

1602-1786 Denmark imposes a trade monopoly on Iceland

1660 Iceland comes fully under Danish rule

1783 Lakagígar eruption

1874 Denmark grants Iceland a constitution and home rule

1918 Iceland becomes a sovereign state

1944 Icelanders vote to terminate union with Denmark. Iceland becomes an independent republic.

Introduction

Years ago, way back in 2010 to be precise, I wound up self-publishing an eBook that I called *The Little Book of the Icelanders*. I had been writing a blog for a few years called "The Iceland Weather Report", which chronicled what it was like to live on the piece of rock in the North Atlantic known as Iceland, and the *Little Book* was intended for readers of that blog. In the book I wrote about the quirks and foibles of the Icelandic people as they appeared to me, a "pseudo-Icelander" who had grown up in another country and returned "home" as a foreign person more than twenty years later. To my surprise and delight, the *Little Book* was well received, and eventually it was released as a traditional hard-cover publication. It has since been translated into French and German, and a Spanish version is due out as I write this.

Right around that time I decided to return to university to finish my undergraduate degree. I took English as a major, and Ethnology/Folkloristics (that's what the University of Iceland calls it) as a minor. The latter included a course with the enticing name "Lice Combs, Chamber Pots and Sex - Customs, Traditions and Daily Life in the Earlier Rural Society of Iceland". The course described life in the Icelandic rural societies of old, and I came to see that, if the Icelanders have quirks today, they had some *serious* quirks back then.

But these weren't merely weird. They were also hilarious. And ingenious. And amazing. In fact I began to gain a new respect and awe for my ancestors, who had found ways to survive under conditions that could cause even the most intrepid adventurer to cower in fear. Moreover, they survived not only physically, but also spiritually and emotionally - soldering bravely on, if not with dignity, then at least with an irrepressible urge to keep on living.

I decided I wanted to write about this. The trouble was, how to get across the remarkable reality of the Icelanders of yore in a comprehensive or linear way? I pondered that for about five minutes, and decided to not even try. I'm not a historian, and there are others who have done a far better job of that than I possibly could. I bow down to them. I also include some of their work in a sources list at the end of this book. Though I must say that I am indebted to one text above all others: the excellent *Íslenzkir þjóðhættir (Icelandic Folkways)*, first published in 1934, which is *the* definitive text on Icelandic customs and traditions in centuries past.

In the end I decided to stick to what I do reasonably well - writing text that is light and fun and easy to read (I hope).

My next conundrum was the time span. Iceland was officially settled in 874, and we're basically looking at the period stretching from then until, oh, about the end of the 19th century. As you can imagine, many things changed during that time ... and yet many things stayed the same. For most of that time Iceland was a colony. For all of that time, it was abjectly poor. I have tried to specify the time in which things happened when I feel that it matters;

otherwise I've left it out. For an overview of Iceland's history, please see the timeline I've provided at the beginning of the book.

A parallel issue was how much detail to include. For example, when writing about the types of light sources used, should I get into the different types of fish oil lamps, the evolution of candle making and the intricacies of candle stick holders throughout the centuries? In cases like those, I chose the option that was likely to keep you, the reader, awake. I may have left out a whole bunch of stuff, but I'd rather have your continued attention than your collective snoring.

I should be very clear on one thing before going further: this book is about the proletariat. The plebs. Granted, "proletariat" referred to just about everybody in Iceland back in the day. There was not much in the way of an upper class. The closest to it would have been the king's cohorts or representatives in Iceland, and the district magistrates and ecclesiastical authorities (bishops and the like), who held a fair amount of sway. Yet even those folks lived in turf houses until well into the 19th century, like everyone else.

I have gone to great lengths to ensure the accuracy of this book, but if there are any errors or omissions, please don't shoot me (or drown me, or make me drink nothing but Brennivín for the rest of my days). Again, I am just a humble layperson trying to tackle a wide and complex subject, and trying to convey my enthusiasm and fascination as best I can in 50 short essays. And hopefully to take you for an enjoyable ride.

1 Turf

So I guess since I'm not going for "comprehensive" or "linear" it's a question of starting somewhere. Anywhere. And since I've just mentioned housing I may as well start with that.

Unlike almost every nation in Europe, Icelanders do not possess proud architecture from their past. Our buildings were made of turf, and unless a farmhouse was kept up with diligent, regular maintenance, within a few years it had inevitably dissolved back into the landscape. On your wanderings in Iceland you may occasionally chance upon some rocks arranged in a semi-organised fashion, overgrown with grass and other vegetation that may or may not have decayed bits of wood somewhere nearby. That would probably be an abandoned turf farm.

The first abodes, in the settlement age, were longhouses anywhere from fifteen to eighty metres long (between sixteen and ninety yards), and five to seven metres wide (five and a half to seven and a half yards). They had one or two entrances, and a long fire in the middle. These houses were apparently pretty common in northern Europe at that time. Gradually this longhouse tradition began to expand as little annexes were added, such as storerooms, a kitchen, a workshop, a room for receiving guests, a WC (!) and - significantly - a room for bathing. By which I mean, a room with hot coals onto which people would throw water to make steam. A sauna, basically.

These annexes were often separate from the main house, until someone figured it would be kind of rad to connect them with a tunnel. This caught on, and those kinds of farms, called *gangnabæir*, "tunnel farms", became all the rage. The tunnel was for the sake of comfort, obviously, since the weather in winter could be a little, um, intense. And folks didn't really relish fighting their way to the sauna wearing nothing but a towel and flip-flops.

Now, being not much more than hillocks in the ground, though with a ceiling height of approximately four metres, these turf farmhouses were a little, shall we say, *challenged* in the daylight department. So at some point someone (maybe the same person who came up with the tunnel idea) figured out that if you had, say, the front of the house made of wood, you could insert a window and get some light in the place.

Stellar though this piece of innovation was, it did have its drawbacks. Mainly that wood paneling at the front of the house meant no insulation (yes, turf did have its advantages, though they were not many) and lack of insulation meant *bloody damn cold*. Consequently the front-panelled farmhouses were far more common in the south than in the north ... on account of the sweltering temperatures, you understand. The tunnel farms tended to be more common in the north, where it was always freezing. (I say this with tongue firmly in cheek, mind. There isn't a vast discrepancy in temperatures between the north and the south of Iceland ... though clearly there was enough to warrant this difference.)

Today the only such farms in existence are those that have been painstakingly reconstructed by the National Museum of Iceland, or similar institutions. And even that only began relatively recently. The reason? When Iceland gained its independence from Denmark, the turf farms came to be seen as symbols of its oppression and poverty. Icelanders were ashamed of them, and therefore they were generally left to rot, or even outright destroyed. They were certainly never thought of with any sort of nostalgia, until the latter part of the 20th century, when people began to accept these abodes as something with intrinsic historical value.

2 Bath parlour

The Icelanders called their sauna room *baðstofa*, or "bath parlour". And lest you're wondering where they got all those coals from ... well, believe it or not, Iceland was reportedly covered in forest back then, and forest meant they quite literally had wood to burn. So those chieftains and their kin could lounge in the sauna all day long if they so desired, without having to worry about freezing to death later (that problem would be passed on to their descendants).

But lo! Just as the Icelanders were getting used to steaming their cares away, the world entered the Little Ice Age and temperatures across the globe took a downturn. Suddenly it was a helluva lot colder in Iceland than it had been. And, most alarmingly, all the wood that had previously been in such vast abundance was gone. Spent. Whittled away in the sauna.

But of course all this didn't happen overnight. When temps first began to drop there were still coals available, and the fire burned happily away in the baðstofa, which was probably pretty well insulated. So people started gravitating over there, not just to have a sauna, but also to warm their toes and fingers by the embers. Gradually it became so cold in other parts of the house that they started sleeping in there, and over time everyone on the farm moved into the baðstofa. It became the centre of the home - the communal living area. It was where people ate, slept, worked, entertained, learned, fucked, peed, shat (at least at night), had babies, died ... where they played out their entire lives, basically.

Oh, and by this time they'd stopped having saunas. That party was over. Done.

The baðstofa was *tiny*. (Well, as living quarters it was - it probably would have done reasonably well as a sauna.) It was approximately four metres wide and seven metres long (four by seven and a half yards). Factor into that beds along both walls, and all the space they had to move around in was a small aisle in the middle, and maybe a small space at the end of the row of beds. Later, some of the *baðstofur* (plural of baðstofa) had a room at one end where the farmer (the head of the house) and his wife slept. The rest of the folks slept together. (Or, well, not *together*. Just ... in one room.)

The main objective in all this, obviously, was to stay warm. That's why people slept two to a bed, and that's why they built the baðstofa above the sheep and cow shed, so the heat from the animals would rise up and wrap the people in its cosy and delicious warmth.

We won't talk about the smell. People bathed maybe once a year (whether they needed to or not), changed their bedding as often, and stashed their chamberpots beneath the bed (though they were generally emptied in the mornings). Add to that the beasts below the floorboards, and the stench was probably a little overpowering, irrespective of what people are able to get used to when needed.

This was compounded by the absence of privacy, the lice that were so aggressive that people often had open lesions on their skin, the lack of daylight and ventilation, the proliferation of insects, death and disease, and the realisation that those conditions would probably not change in your lifetime, and you really have to wonder how the Icelanders managed to keep from collectively marching off the nearest cliff.

3 Stayin' awake

My theory? They remained sane largely due to the *kvöldvaka*. It was their anti-depressant, their Prozac, in the old days.

The word "kvöldvaka" is one of those pesky words that simply cannot be translated into English. A very basic literal translation would be "evening wake", which doesn't make sense, particularly since that's "wake" as in "staying awake", not as in someone-died-and-they-are-lying-in-an-open-casket wake. So we have to resort to a non-literal translation, which might well be: "Anything designed to keep people awake and entertained during those dark evenings in the baðstofa so they could perform their work more efficiently".

It took place during the evenings in winter when everyone at the farm was hanging out in the baðstofa doing their "winter work" - knitting, spinning, carding, tool-making ... basically anything they did with their hands and that could be done indoors.

And yet, even the above definition doesn't do full justice to the role of the kvöldvaka. It was also a time when children were educated - where they were taught to read and write. It was where people told the sorts of stories that became ingrained into their very identities and being, of heroes, gods, trolls, outlaws, hidden people, and things that went bump in the night. Or where they read out loud from whatever books were available on the farm at any given time, giving people a brief respite from their day-to-day slogs. It was where they kept their minds active by making up poetry on the spot, which they called *að kveðast á* - someone would make up the first line of a poem, someone else would make up the next line, and so on. Or someone would recite long, epic poems from memory about Norse gods and kings and everything that constituted good, ethical behaviour, thereby teaching everyone else about good, solid values, as well as about history, geography, their own culture, and other cultures.

In the midst of the losses, the griefs, the hardships of people's day-to-day lives, the stories told at the kvöldvaka provided hope. They spoke of another time and place, of ancestors who were heroes or kings or chieftains (and murderous pillaging Viking raiders, but we won't go there), who had confronted adversity and emerged victorious. Naturally the stories always had a happy ending - or if not, they at least had a moral lesson. Through them, people came to believe that a better life was possible.

Finally, one cannot underestimate the significance of those stories to the upbringing and spiritual development of children. They provided a moral compass and role models where parents so often failed - not because they were bad parents, but because so little time could be devoted to the raising of children. People toiled from morning to night, their time completely taken up by the business of survival. The children were therefore left pretty much to their own devices, and the stories they heard fuelled their imaginations. They learned of noble and valiant heroes who had integrity, who could be admired, and whom they could imitate. Those stories shaped their character, and strengthened their sense of right and wrong.

In short, the kvöldvaka was the cradle of the Icelanders' emotional and spiritual lives, a cultural institution upon which the nation's values rested.

4 Read on

Children largely learned to read during the kvöldvaka. And I would like to say that it was because their parents bore such an intense reverence for the written and spoken word that they could not imagine anything more essential than their offspring learning to make sense of those squiggly symbols that we call letters.

But it was slightly more complex than that.

You see, teaching children to read was not an option, at least not in 18th century Iceland. The national church decreed that everyone had to learn to read, so they could successfully adopt its religious teachings. Not that this was exclusive to Iceland - making people literate was the business of ecclesiastical authorities all over Europe. Still, I don't know the church elsewhere actually made it *obligatory* to teach your kids to read - although I may be wrong.

The enforcement of this decree in Iceland was the responsibility of the local minister. He regularly made the rounds of the humble abodes of his parishioners and tested the children to see if they were up to speed. If he found them lacking he was authorised by law to have them removed from their parents and placed at some other farm where their education would be more attentively seen to. Not surprisingly, children dreaded these visits. Probably for good reason, too, since I'm pretty sure your average minister would have had a limited understanding of dyslexia or other learning disorders, and that children thus afflicted would not have met with a great deal of compassion.

The ultimate test of the children's achievements was the confirmation, which took place in the year when they turned fourteen. This was a major rite of passage, and officially marked a child's transition into adulthood. (The confirmation still exists today but has been turned into a kind of materialistic parody of itself. For one thing, no person of sound mind in our day and age would agree that a child of fourteen should be considered an adult. But it was a different era then, and children grew up far more quickly - mentally, if not physically. I say this because children today go through puberty earlier than their peers in the old days did - likely due to all those improved living conditions. Or something.)

So back in the day, people were officially adults at the ripe old age of fourteen ... albeit adults that had pretty much no authority over their own lives. But at least they could read.

5 Pecking order

Before I go further it might be a good idea to talk about social structure among the common folk in the Iceland of old.

It went something like this: Farmer → Croft Farmer → Freelancer → Farmhand → Dependent of the District → Vagabond.

Farms were grouped into districts called *hreppar*. To qualify as a *hreppur*, a district had to have at least twenty farms known as *lögbýli*, or "legal farms" - so named to differentiate them from the croft farms sometimes situated on their land. The district collected taxes and had various obligations towards its citizens, such as making sure they had a roof over their heads and did not starve to death. They could starve *almost* to death, but not fully. In that sense the hreppur was kind of like a welfare bureau - although a rather ineffective one, it must be said.

THE FARMER was the head of the legal farm. A whole bunch of people lived on a farm, including the farmer's family, farmhands, possibly freelancers and vagabonds on occasion, and dependents of the district.

The concept of personal liberty didn't really exist in the Iceland of old, and the farmer had pretty much full and total control over the people who lived on his farm.

For instance the farmhands were not allowed to leave the farm without the farmer's permission ... although, to be fair, the farmer was not allowed to leave the district either without the express permission of the district administrative officer or the local minister. (God forbid that people just be allowed to wander about at will.) The farmer was entitled to any money that a farmhand in his employ might earn, even if it was earned away from the farm, say in a fishing station somewhere.

So essentially the farmhands had the legal status of children in relation to their farmer-father. In return, the farmer was obliged to treat his farmhand-children well, which meant housing, feeding and clothing them.

Now, you might perhaps think that a farmer would have carved out a pretty secure place for himself in Icelandic society. Not so. He was usually a tenant farmer himself. In fact almost all farmers in Iceland were, and they leased the land on which they lived for a year at a stretch. At the end of that year, the farmer could (and frequently did) move to another farm. He could also be evicted by the landowner. Roughly half of all land in Iceland was owned by wealthy landowners, the other half by the crown and/or the church.

THE CROFT FARMER generally sub-leased a little piece of land from the legal farmer. The legal farmer was officially responsible for the croft farmer's welfare, meaning he had to support the croft farmer if he fell on hard times and ensure that he did not become a burden on the district. In other respects, the croft farmer was free to manage his time and affairs, and that of his family.

FREELANCERS were an interesting class of people. To be viable as such you had to be financially solvent, which in practice meant you had to own the equivalent of ten cows (the currency by which things were measured back then). Make no mistake: this was a hefty sum. To set up your own farm you only had to own the equivalent of three cows, so you can see what this meant. The logic behind it was that your ten cows were like your health and infirmity insurance, since if you were your own boss you had no one (read: no patriarchal farmer figure) to take care of you if you fell on hard times.

On the whole, being a freelancer was pretty sweet, because if you were able to establish yourself as such you could earn a nice sum *and* have the flexibility of doing your own thing - in other words not have to abide by the laws imposed on farmhands. For example if you sold your services during the busiest weeks in the summer - haymaking season - you could earn more money in just that period than a regular farmhand made in a year. The main problem you faced as a freelancer was where to live between jobs ... and some folks got pretty creative when it came to that, as I'll explain later.

FARMHANDS. If you didn't have three cows to start your own farm you had to find yourself a position as a farmhand. That's right. You *had* to have a place on a farm. Once you had it, you were obliged to stay there for a year, but were graciously permitted to move to another farm at the end of that year, provided you had secured yourself a place. This "farmhand year", for lack of a better term, stretched from May to May, and at the end of it there was a four-day period in which people were allowed to move to their new positions. These days were called *fardagar*, "moving days", and as you can probably imagine there was a lot of bustling activity in the Icelandic countryside at that time. Farmhands made up twenty-five percent of the Icelandic population in the 19th century, and people of this rank were not permitted to marry unless they had the financial capacity to start their own farms - which very few people did. And the wage gap sure was alive and well back then ... male farmhands received a wage equal to the value of half a cow per year, while female farmhands received a wage of ... nothing. That's correct. *Nothing*.

DEPENDENTS OF THE DISTRICT. So people were legally obliged to find themselves positions on farms, but alas, it sometimes happened that there were no positions to be had. This was especially true when times were hard, like after the Lakagígar eruption in 1783, which killed about a quarter of the Icelandic population, wiped out about eighty percent of all sheep, and fifty percent of other livestock. People who could not find positions had nowhere to go, and became welfare cases. These "dependents of the district", as they were called, were then randomly placed on farms in their area, and the district paid for their upkeep. And if you think that people could just kick back and have a top nice time of it as they collected their welfare ... think again. That upkeep the district paid turned into debt that the poor hapless dependents were required to pay back. Just *how* that was supposed to happen was a mystery ... remember that female farmhands earned no money. And until such a time that they did repay their debt they were virtual prisoners of the district. They were not permitted to marry for the next ten years, for instance, unless their debt was settled.

VAGABONDS. These were the people who did not fit any of the above categories. I've decided to devote a whole separate section to them later in this book because, well, they're kind of fascinating.

6 Waking sticks

By far the most important time of year for indoor work (and therefore the kvöldvaka) was the week leading up to Christmas. People had to work overtime to get everything done at that time, not only so they could give each other half-decent prezzies, but also because the farmers to whom they were accountable had frequently accumulated debts with the merchants in town. To offset those debts, the farmers needed to make deposits by the end of the year, and these deposits were in the form of goods. Consequently their farmhands had to bust their butts in the handiwork department in the days leading up to Christmas.

(Incidentally, it is very likely that this is where the legend of the Yule Cat originated. If you're not familiar

with the dreaded Cat, it is the pet of an old ogre named Grýla, who lives in a cave and eats naughty children. Legend has it that the Yule Cat will appear and *eat* any person who does not get a new item of clothing for Christmas. This is called, in Icelandic, *að fara í jólaköttinn*, literally "to go into the Yule Cat", and figuratively "to become the prey of the Yule Cat". As it happens, Grýla is also the mother of the thirteen Icelandic Yule Lads, which I guess you could call the Icelandic equivalent of Santa Claus, except they tend to be mischievous and nasty, which probably tells you a fair bit about the nature of Icelandic society back in the day. But I digress.)

Yet folks are human, as we know, and tend to get sleepy even when they're being told thrilling stories about ghosts and hidden people and bloodthirsty mass-murdering early settlers, so someone had to invent something to keep them working even when they were on the verge of nodding off.

Enter the *vökustaurar*, literally "waking sticks". You know when someone casually remarks that they need to put toothpicks in their eyelids to stay awake? Well, according to *Íslenzkir þjóðhættir* the Icelanders actually did that. They had these little wooden sticks with a small slit on one side that were sort of split down the middle, and they made it so painful for people to close their eyes that they had no choice but to stay awake, knitting or carding or spinning or doing whatever they were doing, all because grabbing a wee shut-eye *hurt too damn much*.

Those of you who have read the first *Little Book* will know that Icelanders like to work in spurts, everyone working in unison like a well-oiled machine until the work gets done. I have heard it said that this is coded into the Icelanders' DNA because of all the occasions when fishing boats would come in with the catch and people would have to go down to the docks and move like gangbusters to preserve it. But now I'm thinking it's much more likely that it was conditioned into the fabric of the Icelandic nation with those little toothpick-like thingies that pinched your eyelids if you were about to fall asleep.

7 Let there be light

I'm sure you realise that normal daylight did not suffice to adequately illuminate the Icelandic turf houses of old, particularly not in the winter. Other light providers had to come into play. And naturally folks did not have the luxury that we have, of light at the flick of a switch. Back then light providers were enormously precious, and people went to vast lengths to conserve them.

So how *did* people light their cosy turf farmhouses? Well, apart from your basic fire, the two main providers of light were candles and fish oil lamps. And both presented a functional challenge.

The main problem with the candles, at least initially, was that they were supremely expensive. The first ones were made of beeswax, that had to be imported.

Consequently they were used only in churches during special ceremonies. However, around the year 1400, people figured out that you could make candles out of tallow (animal fat). This changed everything. Candles could now be manufactured in their own kitchens, so to speak, and used for pretty much any occasion. Even so, they remained fairly precious (tallow wasn't an inexhaustible resource), and possessing your very own candle was kind of a big deal. For that reason they were extremely popular Christmas gifts. As in, *extremely* popular. As in, pretty much the only Christmas gift worth giving (with all due respect to mittens, sweaters, and the like). You see, having your own candle meant that you could read or do whatever you wanted to that required light, when you pleased and where you pleased - you didn't have to do it in unison with all the other people in the baðstofa. A candle was a small chunk of liberation.

As for the oil lamps, they were initially nothing more than small, flat stones - pebbles, really - with an indentation in the middle into which the fish oil was poured. The wick, stuck into the oil and then lit, was made of cotton grass, which grows in relative abundance in Iceland. As you can imagine, these didn't provide a huge amount of light. Later, proper oil lamps made of metal, which also burned fish oil, were introduced. This fish oil reportedly had a disgusting odour, adding to the olfactory calamity that already existed inside the baðstofa.

Kerosene lamps were not introduced to Iceland until the late 19th century and were met with a great deal of suspicion. They gave off so much light. *Too* much light. It just wasn't right. Consequently they were denounced as a frivolous luxury that wasted fuel and furthermore could easily burn down the house (had it not been made mostly of turf). Candles, on the other hand, were the real deal, and had proven their dependability. Presumably no candle had ever caused a fire in the Iceland of old.

8 Ceremony of light-time

As I was saying, these light providers were incredibly precious. So precious that there was a small ceremony each time the light was lit during the darkest time. That time even had its own name: *ljósatími*, literally "light time". The ljósatími, which lasted from around six to ten in the evening, usually began in mid-September, coinciding with a specific event such as the first sheep round-up, and lasted until approximately mid-March.

This light-lighting ceremony in the evenings was invariably preceded by the so-called *rökkurstund*, or "twilight hour". This was the interval between when it had become too dark to work without light, and before the lamp - or other light source - was formally lit. It had a two-fold function: to conserve the light source (after all, it wasn't pitch dark yet), and also to provide a time of rest and repose. If people wanted to talk during the rökkurstund, they had to talk quietly. Children were sent outside to play if the weather permitted, or, if it did not, they had to pass the time quietly with their toys in the corner of the baðstofa.

The rökkurstund lasted for about an hour. After that, to signal the beginning of the evening's activities in the baðstofa, the mistress of the house would formally light the lamp. If she was indisposed, one of the female farmhands to whom she had entrusted the task would do so. In other words, it wasn't done by just anybody, and it generally wasn't done by men. The domestic sphere, even back then, was primarily a woman's domain.

9 Let there be daylight

The absence of light was not only a problem in the winter, mind. Given the materials out of which the houses were built, it was also a challenge in the summer. The turf walls of the farmhouses were thick and therefore pretty good at preventing drafts and keeping in warmth, but that also meant that they kept *out* the daylight, and *in* air that was rancid and stale.

A solution had to be found, and that solution came in the form of holes made in the roof of the baðstofa. Sometimes there was only one hole, and sometimes there were two. Obviously they couldn't just be left open, though, because, you know, rain and snow and wind and sleet, and in those days glass windows were way *way* out of the price range of ordinary folk.

So those crafty Nicelanders came up with something called a *skjár*, or "screen". Basically it consisted of a thin membrane made of the amniotic sac of a cow, stretched over and fastened to the wooden ring from a barrel. Whenever a cow calved, great care was taken to keep the amniotic sac as whole as possible. It was then washed, stretched out and dried, then wet again and stretched onto the barrel ring. This circular "window" was then stuffed into the hole in the roof. If it snowed so much that the skjár became covered over (thereby preventing daylight from entering) it was removed (from the inside), the snow brushed off, and then re-inserted. If it was really cold and there was a lot of frost, half- or one-inch thick slabs of ice would be placed on top of the opening, and the snow packed carefully around the edges. Either that or the hole, with the screen in it, would be filled with snow in the evening in order to keep in the warmth, and then uncovered in the morning.

Pretty ingenious, wouldn't you agree?

When someone in the baðstofa died (which happened as a matter of course) it was considered essential to re-move the skjár closest to the bed of the deceased so that the soul could escape. The skjár then had to be re-in-serted *upside-down* to prevent the soul from coming back into the house and re-entering the body. In the unfortu-nate event that this happened, said body could be used to do annoying stuff like haunting, harassing, mauling or killing people. And no one wanted that.

10 The high risk of pregnancy

But hey, I wasn't planning to talk about death quite yet. Rather, let's talk about birth. More specifically: crazy superstitions relating to birth.

Back in the days when Iceland was hopelessly poor, folks typically set out to have somewhere in the ballpark of six to sixteen children. (Although given that most people did not marry until around thirty years of age, they presumably would have had to turbo-charge their efforts.) Half of those children might reach adulthood - that is, if they managed to enter the world at all. Being pregnant in those days was a pretty risky proposition, you see. And to minimise risk, a woman needed to steer clear of many, many things, such as:

Eating with a spoon that had a cleft in it, or her child would be born with a harelip.

Running while pregnant, or her child would be prone to dizzy spells.

Looking over the edge of anything at high elevation, or her child would have a fear of heights.

Stepping over a cat in heat, or her child would be born an idiot or at the very least a very unfortunate person.

Pissing in the moonlight, or her child would be born insane.

Eating seal flippers, or her child would be born with flippers.

Eating the soft palate of an animal head, or her child would have a cleft palate.

... And so on. And on. Many, *many* things.

Now, let's say that a woman was extremely, ridiculously careful, and did everything by the book to ensure that her child would turn out absolutely flawless. Ach, alas. There were still loads of things beyond her control that might severely affect her child. For instance:

If someone came into a house with a sack on their back and did not put down the sack outdoors, the child would turn out to be a cripple.

If someone came into a house wearing skates or crampons, the child would have skates or crampons for feet.

... Just as an example.

And that wasn't all. There were plenty of superstitions surrounding the actual birth, too. A woman must not, for example:

Walk under the rafters of a newly-raised house, or she would not be able to deliver the child unless rafters were raised over her. (Which would presumably take far too much time and both would die.)

Walk underneath a clothes line, or the child would be born with the umbilical cord around its neck and would therefore be strangled.

Lie on a duvet of ptarmigan feathers, or the child would just not be born.

A woman *should*, on the other hand, lie on a bearskin

while delivering the baby, because then the child would receive a *bjarnaryl*, or "bear warmth", and would never in its life be cold.

It's difficult to know just where all those superstitions came from. However, pregnancy is a state that anthropologists call "liminality", taken from the Latin word "limen", meaning threshold. Essentially this is a period of transition, or change, in which a person is on the threshold to what they are about to become, but cannot go back to what they previously were. An "in-between-time", as it were. Applied to this particular instance, it means that the mother is no longer an un-pregnant woman, but has not yet become an "ex-pregnant woman" (or, put more plainly, a *mama*).

I mention this because liminality is a state that is known to generate a huge amount of superstition. It's on account of the uncertainty, you see - people trying to grasp at some sort of security straw, hoping to influence or control the Great Big Unknown by carrying out this or that superstition. At a time when only about half of children lived to see adulthood, it is easy to see why this was important. Which is probably why there were infinitely more active superstitions surrounding pregnancy and childbirth at that time than there are today.

11 A child makes it into the world!

If a woman managed to get to the actual birth of her child without a serious calamity taking place, a midwife was commonly called on to assist. Prior to 1760, every church parish in the country had one appointed mid-wife, and it was the role of the local minister to "train" her. Effectively this meant that he taught her a bunch of prayers to recite over the childbearing woman, depending on the condition of mother and child in any given instance.

When the baby had successfully been ejected into the world it was wrapped in a blanket and something stuck into its mouth. That "something" was generally not its mother's nipple, as Icelanders were not big on breast-feeding in those days. Instead it was usually a piece of cloth wrapped around some food-related matter that could easily be inserted into the baby's mouth for it to suck on, and from which it was to gather its nourishment. This might be, say, dried fish that an adult person had chewed and then spat into the cloth.

(And they wonder why half of the children died.)

After the birth, the mother stayed in bed for about a week. (None of this hustling her out of the hospital within twenty-four hours back then.) The local women would then come visit and bring something for the new mother - often some type of food, like meat, bread, butter, sausage, or smoked sheep belly.

Not that the birth meant an end to all superstitions. Goodness, no. The placenta still needed to be disposed of. It was considered holy, and folks believed that it contained a part of the child's soul. Obviously, then, you couldn't just toss it out the door, because bad spirits could get a hold of it. Neither could you give it to the dog, because if an animal ate the placenta, that animal would follow the child around forevermore (and though children tend to like dogs, you probably wouldn't want one shadowing you until you died). Even if you buried the placenta, animals could still dig it out of the ground and eat it. If that option was selected (and occasionally it was), people would usually put a heavy stone on top of the burial place so no animal could get at it.

The most auspicious thing was to burn the placenta. If you did that, a light or a star would follow the child around for the rest of its life. Which was infinitely preferable to, say, the black dog with the fleas.

When a woman got out of bed after giving birth, she had to put on new shoes. If she put on old shoes, she would get worse again and have to spend more time in bed. And in cases where the placenta had been buried, when she first got out of bed she had to step on the stone that had been placed on top of it, for some inexplicable reason.

Naturally no sex-related act (which pregnancy indisputably is) could be without its two bits of shame, courtesy of the church. After she gave birth, a woman was considered unclean, and ideally should not leave the farm until she had been "led to church", as it was called. (Though how exactly she was supposed to be led to church without first leaving the farm is a bit nebulous.) For that she was supposed to put on her best clothes and jewellery (if she had any - jewellery, that is) and go and stand in front of the church door. The minister would come to the door, recite a little sermon over the woman, presumably in the most magnanimous fashion, and then lead her personally to her seat. When that was done, she was "cleansed" and could begin to attend church again in a regular manner.

12 Naming jinx

By law, children had to be baptised in a church, except if someone's life was at risk. If the baptism didn't take place within seven days, the parents of the child were levied a fine. Complying with this rule could obviously be difficult, particularly in winter when the weather was frequently crazy and roads and mountain routes impassable. Even so, people were pretty conscientious about this, packing up their infants and heading out on the sometimes lengthy journey to the church - even if it meant putting the life of the child in danger. Indeed, infants often didn't make it to the church, as they had died along the way.

Icelandic parents have a tendency to name their children

after someone - whether it is a relative, a good friend, or someone who has appeared to them in a dream *að vitja nafns* (explained in the first *Little Book*). They call this *að skíra í höfuðið á einhverjum*, literally "to baptise into the head of someone". So let's say the parents named their child Ljótur into the head of its grandfather, and it was a name they treasured. If Ljótur died, it might be tempting for the parents to pass on the name to the next son that was born to them. But! This was strictly inadvisable. If they did (the superstition went), that child would most likely die, too.

However, if they were really, *really* hung up on that name, all was not lost ... the best thing in that case was to let two or three children be born in between, before attempting the name again. For added safety it was considered best to throw another name into the mix. Like, say, Ljótur *Ormur* Illugason. That would likely be enough to break the jinx (or so they believed).

13 Battle over the young soul

It was absolutely essential to keep a vigilant watch over the children when they were small, and not just because otherwise they might bump their heads or fall into a river. No, it was essential because there were enemies lurking in the shadows, just waiting for their chance to snatch the child away. And when I say "enemies" I am thinking of two in particular: the dreaded Lucifer himself, and those dastardly hidden people.

The Lucifer thing was a no-brainer. Everybody knew that he was always skulking around waiting for a chance to possess children and turn them into horrible apparitions. This was supposedly pretty easy to do before the child was baptised and the evil spirit with which it was born was still living inside of it. You see, the folks of old believed that a child was born inherently evil, and if that child died before it was baptised, it would get no rest in heaven. Similarly, if a child was *borið út* - a compound verb meaning "left outside somewhere to die" (apparently this was common enough in the Iceland of old to warrant its own verb), an evil spirit would inevitably enter it (... wait, wasn't the child supposed to have been born with one of those already?), after which it would proceed to wail and moan incessantly and generally wreak havoc and misery on its immediate surroundings.

That was Lucifer and his minions. Then there were the hidden folk, who had slightly different objectives. They were constantly trying to get a hold of human children so they could replace them with decrepit old people, whom they would "knead together" as Jónas Jónasson puts it in his book *Íslenzkir þjóðhættir*, until they were the size of infants. They would make the old fogeys look like infants, too, but the problem was that they never grew, just became mentally, um, challenged and were generally a pain in the posterior in every respect.

One way to help keep the children safe from these heinous predators was to make the sign of the cross over them. Yet this wasn't entirely foolproof because some hidden people were also Christians, so it didn't bother them in the least. A better strategy was to douse the infants' heads so well with holy water during the baptism that some of it went into their eyes. This is because people believed that children were born clairvoyant (and evil ... an alarming combination), and the holy water removed their ability to see the hidden people. Consequently it became more difficult for the hidden folk to lure the children away, since they weren't visible to them. If they nevertheless *did* manage to lure a child away, it was considered to be the fault of the minister, who clearly had not done a proper job with the baptism.

14 A brief lecture about elves

I hope you'll allow me a momentary digression here. We'll return to our regular programming in a minute.

I'm sure you've heard the stories: Icelanders believe in elves, won't build anything without first checking whether there are elves living there, go around knocking on boulders to say hello to the elves, make whole maps of elf colonies, and blah-de-blah.

The international media loves to chew on this stuff, and the Icelandic tourist industry loves to feed it to them.

Well, I'm here to tell you: it's a crock of poo.

"But!" I hear you say breathlessly. "There was this study that showed that Icelanders most definitely do believe in elves. I read about it in Vanity Fair [or insert name of other sophisticated media outlet here]."

Sure, ok. I will grant that there was a study. And allegedly, in this study, some amazingly high proportion of respondents said they believed in elves. However, and this is important: nobody ever tells you how the question was worded. The question was *not*: "Do you believe in elves?" The question was: "Would you be prepared to absolutely rule out the existence of elves?"

And some really high proportion said that they would absolutely not be prepared to rule out the existence of elves. Because, well, we don't know, right? I mean, if I was asked "Would you absolutely rule out that the Kardashian family is a pack of zombies?" I would probably answer, "No, I would not absolutely rule it out". Because what the hell do I know about zombies and the way they might choose to infiltrate mainstream media? Not a thing.

That doesn't mean I believe zombies are real, though. (In fact, what it probably means is that I have no freaking idea what makes the Kardashians so incredibly appealing ... but that's not the point.)

And please don't get me started on those few Icelandic folks who run "elf schools" or offer elf tours to hapless tourists, who are led around the elf grounds and told where the elves live, where they go to church, where they do their grocery shopping, where they work out, and where they do whatever "elves" get up to in their daily lives. Sometimes the guides even have conversations with elves, which the poor tourists don't see because THEY'RE NOT FREAKING THERE.

Run a poll asking, "Do you think the people who offer elf tours to tourists are weirdos who may or may not believe in elves but definitely believe in making money off tourists?", and I'm willing to bet that at least ninety-four percent of Icelanders would offer a resounding yes. If they were asked why they thought that, they'd probably say: "Because there is no such thing as elves".

Yes, there have been instances of roads being diverted around some big boulder or other because there were allegedly elves living in there and making the construction equipment break down. But as far as I'm aware no roads have been diverted for a good long while.

And by the way there is no fundamental difference between the terms "elves" and "hidden people". In Icelandic folklore they are basically the same phenomenon, and the terms are used pretty much interchangeably. Still, to me the term "elves" conjures up thoughts of diminutive green-clad persons with pointy hats. This is vastly different from the elves, or hidden people, of Icelandic lore, who were almost always tall, regal, self-possessed, and a lot better looking than the snivelling mortals all around them. Naturally. After all, what else would you expect from creatures that can knead old people into infants?

15 Those crafty hidden folk and their opulent lives

Don't ask me why, but if old folk stories are any indication the hidden people very often had a bone to pick with the human folk. This was usually because the humans hadn't deigned to do their bidding, which usually meant had not come to their aid in their hour of need. For instance a hidden woman would be giving birth, and a mortal woman would be needed immediately because things were going south at breakneck speed. Hidden women had birthing problems with alarming frequency, it seems ... though, on reflection, perhaps not with any more frequency than ordinary women at the time. Still, one thing is sure: they had a lot of faith in the mortal women's abilities to steer things in the right direction.

The hidden folk, according to legend, lived inside boulders or hillocks, sometimes very close to the abodes of humans. The deal was that they could see the humans, but the humans could only see the hidden people if they wanted to be seen. When they did want to be seen (for the reason above, for example) they usually appeared to the human in a dream. If the human complied with the hidden person's request they were usually handsomely rewarded, for example with a consistently good harvest for the rest of their lives. If they did not, they incurred the wrath of the hidden person, and some great misfortune or other would befall them.

Sometimes when hidden people abducted mortal children and brought them up as their own, those children would re-appear in the human world as adolescents or adults, and successfully continue on with their lives. Here it should be noted that the hidden people did not always leave a shrivelled-up changeling behind ... sometimes they just took the human children without leaving anything.

Hundreds of stories of interactions between hidden people and humans exist, and it is not hard to conceive of the purpose they served. Stories about hidden people abducting children could easily have been a grief-stricken parent's way of coping with a child's unexpected and tragic disappearance. Stories of the *ljúf- lingar*, hidden men who became lovers of mortal women - more on them in a moment - no doubt reflected an intense longing for love and gentleness that most women lacked in their lives. These stories also provided an escape from a harsh and unforgiving reality. The hidden people always led vastly better lives than the humans did. They wore stunning clothes with delicate embroidery, made of opulent fabrics. Their homes were filled with tapestries, plush upholstery and precious metals. They inhabited a world of beauty and luxury that was almost close enough to touch, but which humans could not access - only escape to in their thoughts and dreams.

16 Mountain dairy

Any farm that relied on sheep for its survival (read: every single farm in the country) had a special structure located some distance from the farm itself, called a *sel*, or mountain dairy. These were small, rudimentary structures - little more than stone walls with a makeshift roof, really - located close to the mountain pastures, where the sheep and sometimes cows (if the farm was so prosperous as to have cows) were kept during the summer. These pastures were usually far more verdant and lush than the ones closer to home (besides the fact that the fields close to the farm had to be reserved for haymaking), so that's where the livestock was herded.

At least two people from the farm were routinely sent to spend the summer at the sel. One of those was a shepherd - very often a child or adolescent (you'll recall that children became adults at fourteen, so an adolescent was more like our tweens) who was responsible for watching over the sheep and herding them into a pen at least once a day for milking. The other person was the *matselja*, or "sel food woman" (those prosaic Icelanders!), who was

responsible for milking the sheep and producing food from the milk - generally butter and *skyr* (an Icelandic dairy product similar to a thick yoghurt). Someone would be sent every few days to fetch the produce and take it back to the farm, where it was either eaten or preserved for the winter.

Now, we might be forgiven for thinking that life in the sel was excruciatingly dull, but ... well, maybe not. Thing is, the *matseljur* (that's the plural of matselja) sometimes got pregnant up there. Obviously the shepherds were not to blame (one would hope - given their age), so the question was: *who*?

Answer: the ljúflingar, lovers of mortal women from among the hidden folk population.

Or at least that's what people were saying.

Apparently, these sensitive men - *ljúflingur* means "a gentle man", not to be confused with "a gentleman" - not only made love to the mortal women and got them pregnant, but were also there in the sel to assist during the child's delivery. Still, it was a doomed kind of love, what with the man being hidden and everything, so the woman generally returned to the farm with the child and carried on with her life. However, the ljúflingur (according to the stories) would be unable to forget his mortal woman from the sel, and typically returned many years later, hoping to revive the romance, by which time the child was grown and the sel woman married. This, however, tended to end badly for the ljúflingur, as he would generally wind up dying in the process.

(And you thought trashy Harlequin romances were invented in the 20th century? Ha, NO.)

In some stories, however, the hidden man would take the child with him and raise it in the hidden world. In still others, the child was born in the sel and left outside to die, resulting in the sel becoming haunted.

In our day and age, it is easy to dismiss those stories as fantasies conjured up by women who craved love, tenderness and romance in a world starkly devoid of all those. But it might be more sinister than that. I think we can safely rule out the involvement of supernatural beings, since, as we know, hidden people don't exist and therefore do not go around knocking up women. We can therefore assume that these women became pregnant through their entanglements with some very real mortals - gentle or not. They might have been outlaws who lived in the mountains, or men from nearby farms. Wherever they came from, and whatever their involvement (rape is one possible scenario), we know that there were harsh punishments doled out for having children out of wedlock. It is highly probable, therefore, that tales of the gentle lovers from the hidden world were made up to avoid punishment in the very real physical one.

Incidentally, the word "ljúflingur" is still very much a part of the Icelandic lexicon, but these days it is used to describe (mortal) men who are kind, gentle, and liked by most people.

17 Spring

After being cooped up in their turf houses all winter in the dark, it is easy to imagine the sense of longing that the Icelanders must have felt for spring and summer.

Back then the year was divided into only two seasons: summer and winter. That was according to the old Icelandic calendar, which is still observed today, though in a less official capacity than before. The First Day of Summer fell - and still falls - on the last Thursday in April each year. Back then it was a festive day of celebration - and as a testament to its importance it is still a public holiday today. There was a superstition attached to it (quelle surprise), which held that if winter and summer "froze together" - that is, if there was frost during the night between those two days - then the summer would be good. This belief is still very much a part of the day's festivities, although today it is certainly more for amusement than scientific observation - kind of like the groundhog seeing its shadow in North America.

Some years, summer (otherwise known as "spring") was a long time coming, with the weather staying cold well into the season that today we *do* think of as summer. Sometimes the pack ice, which the Icelanders refer to as *landsins forni fjandi* - "the country's ancient enemy", would drift precariously close to shore. This was Bad, not only because it made fishing impossible and occasionally brought polar bears from the Arctic, but also because when the wind blew across it, it caused the air to cool drastically. This had some pretty serious consequences, like that the grass in the fields wouldn't grow. Consequently the haymaking would be severely impacted, which obviously was disastrous because what were the animals going to eat all winter?

A major concern for farmers at this time of year was getting their animals out of sheds and into the fields for grazing, since by then the hay from the previous summer was inevitably almost all gone. And yet this had to be carefully timed because if the animals were put out too soon they could perish if an unexpected blizzard blew in - which could easily happen, what with Iceland's capricious weather conditions at that (and any) time of year.

The main chore during the spring season was to work the big pile of manure that had been shovelled out of the shed during the winter. Manure, of course, was far more than just a pile of poop to the Icelanders of old. One, it was a fertiliser for the fields, and two, it largely replaced firewood, which was virtually nonexistent for centuries, as we know. When the Icelanders burned manure in the hearth they tended to hang meat above it for preservation. This resulted in smoked meat (obviously), and this *taðreykt* - "manure smoked" - meat is considered a delicacy today, as it was then. Come Christmas, when Icelanders traditionally like to eat smoked lamb, taðreykt is what you want to look for, because it is the best.

18 Making hay

With spring tasks out of the way, the Icelanders geared up for the biggest job of the year: the haymaking. In fact this job was so big that an entire month in the old Icelandic calendar was named after it: Heyannir, literally "hay busy-ness".

The haymaking officially began at the end of July, when the blowballs had formed on the dandelions. This work was executed in systematic fashion: 1) the men went ahead and cut the grass with a scythe, 2) the women and children followed, raking the cut grass into neat rows.

Apparently the pinnacle of humiliation for the menfolk was if the women or children caught up to them. Naturally, then, the men busted their butts to make sure they were well in front. If the women managed to catch up to them it was either called *að raka þá upp að rassi*, "raking them up to their asses", or *að gelda þá*, "to castrate them". Whoa. Not hard to imagine how much male pride hinged on this, then. In some instances the men were even known to grab the women's rakes and snap them in two - particularly if the women were making fun of them, which apparently was part of the game.

After being raked into rows, the grass was turned over and then over again to dry, while everyone begged and prayed that it wouldn't rain. When it was dry (and "grass" had turned into "hay") it was bundled up in bales that were put on horses and transported back to the farms. A hundred bales transported was considered a decent day's work.

A major challenge in this whole haymaking business was stashing the hay so that it would stay dry and thus fit for animal consumption. Proper barns for storing were a major luxury, and very few farms had them. And boy, how easily that hay could turn bad - like if it became wet it could wind up toxic, and if toxic hay was fed to the animals they'd die. Similarly, the hay could become toxic if a dead mouse or other small animal got inside and started to rot.

On the other hand, if the stack of hay became too hot in the middle it could self-ignite. Obviously that had to be prevented. One way to do so (or so people believed) was to place the head of a dead horse in the middle of the stack of hay. How this would *not* poison the hay while a dead mouse *would* poison the hay is a leap in logic of which I am simply not capable. The last time I checked, the head of a horse qualified as a dead animal.

Given that the haymaking was such a crucial task, it was imperative to get it done as quickly and efficiently as possible. This is where the aforementioned freelancers came in. They hired themselves out during the haymaking season, and could apparently make some excellent dosh doing so. But only if they were male. The glass ceiling was very much alive and well in the Iceland of old, and women earned a paltry one-third of what the men earned. (No wonder the menfolk became so humiliated if the women caught up to them.) And there was no slacking off when it came to the work. Folks pulled eighteen-hour days, quitting at 11 pm and getting up at 4 am. Wimps need not apply.

19 And of course, those ubiquitous superstitions

So haymaking was immensely important, and its success hinged on a number of things beyond human control. We know what that meant, right? Yep: *breeding ground for superstition*.

For instance, haymaking could never begin on a Monday. If you wanted a good crop you had to begin on a Friday or Saturday. As far as I know there was no sound logic to this, but I have heard the following explanation proposed: haymaking could not begin on a Monday because the work was so physically taxing that after the first day or two people were barely able to move. Hence a Friday beginning was auspicious - that way people worked Friday and Saturday, had Sunday off to rest, and could return with a vengeance on Monday. (Having of course spent Sunday resting their weary bones on those oh-so comfortable wooden church pews.)

Also, haymaking should begin under a waxing moon. That way the hay would last longer. (For that I have no explanation whatsoever and can't even speculate.)

Another superstition concerned the so-called *álagablettir*, literally "spell spots", areas that allegedly had some kind of spell on them and which you should absolutely, definitively, never ever mow. If you did, something really bad would happen, like the farmhouse would catch on fire, the best dairy cow would die, or you would be forced to eat only putrid shark for the rest of your life (not really). Bizarrely, sometimes those spell spots were right smack in the middle of a field, and would have the most juicy, verdant grass on them - but heaven forbid that you should touch it. Sometimes they had some connection to the hidden folk, like being on top of hillocks inside which hidden people were believed to be living. Sometimes they were on top of an ancient burial place of some chieftain or other, who would surely rise from the dead and slaughter your whole family if you mowed the grass on his grave.

Lastly (but not exhaustively, for there are lots more that we don't have time for here), it was a big no-no to take the last armful of hay with you when you were done. It had to be left behind. Either that, or burned. The reason was simple: you had to show God (or whatever powers were up there watching, and judging) that you weren't greedy. That you wouldn't take everything. That you were humble and gracious enough to leave a little behind.

20 Kiddie workers

Back in the day, everyone had to work, and work hard. Men, women ... and children, from about the age of five.

In the winter, the children did whatever was within their capacity - working the wool, tending to animals, emptying the chamberpots, or whatever. My grandmother, for example, used to tell us about being sent outside in bitter cold and frost at the age of seven to clean the household spittoons in a nearby brook. Her family had been dissolved when her father drowned (that's what normally happened when the man of the house died) and my grandmother was in foster care. More on that later.

As I mentioned earlier, children were often put to work watching over the sheep in the mountain pastures in the summer. They were usually about seven or eight years old when this started, and sometimes even younger. It is hard to imagine today, sending such a small child out alone to spend entire nights (yes) on the edge of the highlands, those dreaded places that everyone feared, as they were believed to be haunted by ghosts and evil apparitions. To say nothing of the outlaws that lived there, who had usually committed some heinous crime or other and had been banished from society as a result.

All this struck terror in the hearts of children, as you can likely imagine. All winter long during the *kvöldvökur* (plural of kvöldvaka) they had listened to stories of ghosts and outlaws, and even though the summer nights were bright, they were only really bright in the days around the summer solstice. Otherwise there was always dusk in the middle of the night, and such twilight hours could easily strike immense fear in the hearts of the little kiddies, of what might lie in the shadows.

Exacerbating this was the fact that the demands made on children were incredibly harsh. If they performed badly, they were often severely reprimanded. And by "performed badly" I mean that they might doze off so that the sheep would wander away, or fall prey to predators like foxes, or even hawks. "Losing" an animal like that often resulted in cruel physical punishment for the child.

All that said, watching over the sheep was not something that all children dreaded. In some instances the demands on the youngsters were not so severe. They were not always made to spend entire nights in the mountain pastures, for instance. Sometimes they only had to stay there during the day, and then they often enjoyed being on their own, letting their imaginations run wild in their own little world, playing with the lambs, or whatever struck their fancy. Indeed, it was often far preferable to being under the watchful eyes of the adults back at the farm, who more often than not had some chore or other for them to perform.

21 Whipped into love

Speaking of punishment, when the children in the Iceland of old were reprimanded, it could be pretty horrific.

Íslenzkir þjóðhættir describes the treatment of children in no uncertain terms, claiming that the work ethic imposed on them was so extreme that many of them never reached a full level of maturity. They had become physically disabled before they even reached adulthood. Discipline was merciless, and no allowance was made for any shortcomings. When the children failed to measure up they were slapped on the face so hard that they bled. They were also whipped daily with brushwood. "This made the children obstinate and cold, cultivated in them stubbornness and deceit, and ruined their minds," writes the book's author Jónas Jónasson. He should know, having been both a minister of the church and a teacher.

Perverse as it may seem, this abuse did not spring from hatred, but from love. Clearly bereft of psychological insight, folks believed that this harsh treatment of children was the best way to make them into strong adults. As a rule, people were made to believe that God was a merciless tyrant and that committing any sin would bring on the full weight of His condemnation, thus propelling them into hell and damnation for eternity. This "fear of God" was designed to frighten people out of committing sin.

(Incidentally, I'm pretty sure this way of thinking was not confined to Iceland, but was common practice in Europe and elsewhere.)

Similarly, children were supposed to be frightened out of their mischief and bad behaviour. "Children should be whipped into love" was a common idiom of the time. The church preached that people should "kiss the rod" of the Lord - meaning the rod with which they were whipped. Thus children were often made to literally kiss the wand of brushwood after they had been whipped with it.

There was in this a brief respite, in that beatings stopped during Lent. But it was short-lived, since punishment for all the "sins" committed during that period was saved up for Good Friday, when "payment" was due. In that way children were literally and quite intentionally made to mirror the plight of Christ.

Such beatings were especially common among children who were dependents of the district - the so-called *niðursetningar*, who had been fostered out. They suffered a multitude of abuse. Also, in families where there were many children, some of them held favour with their parents, while others did not. The ones that did not were called *olnbogabörn* - literally "elbow children". (Why this term I don't know.) Finally, stepchildren were commonly mistreated ... which shouldn't come as a surprise to anyone who has ever read a fairy tale.

22 The farmers who rowed

But let us move on to something else entirely: the Icelanders' longstanding relationship with the sea.

The *Book of Settlements* tells the story of Hrafna Flóki, one of the original settlers, who arrived in Iceland at Barðaströnd, on the West Fjords. At that time the sea was teeming with fish, and old Flóki went hog wild, shovelling seafood into his nets like there was no tomorrow.

This kept him so busy, in fact, that he completely forgot about tomorrow - that is, the vital task of harvesting hay for his animals so they wouldn't starve to death in the winter. Or maybe he thought he'd reached the land of eternal sunshine and verdant fields - after all, the place was covered in forest back then, or so we've been led to believe.

In any case, he failed to make the necessary arrangements to keep his livestock alive, so soon afterward he moved on, undoubtedly cursing the Land of Ice profusely until the end of his days.

Now, given the amazing bounty of the sea, it seems a little odd that fishing didn't catch on properly in Iceland until several centuries after Flóki had made his grumbling exit. Perhaps his story was such a shocking lesson to posterity that people didn't even try to follow his example, or perhaps it was because they knew that the sea is a treacherous place and the waters around Iceland are especially dangerous and unpredictable.

Whatever the cause, Iceland remained primarily an agricultural society for a very long time, or until farmers finally came to the realisation that they could supplement their income very handsomely by fishing.

But this lucrative activity was soon subject to stringent laws and regulations. Not just anyone could hop in a boat and go out fishing (much like today, though for a different reason). If you wanted to fish legitimately you had to be in possession of land, and that land had to border the sea.

So not all farmers qualified, but those who did soon began to set up little fishing stations next to the seashore. If these were near the farm, they were called *heimaver*, or "home station". If they were far away, they were called *útver*, or "out station" - essentially camps for people who couldn't go home in the evenings because of the distance.

Initially, these out stations were really unpleasant. They consisted of ramshackle structures where the fishermen slept in makeshift beds, among their fishing gear and clothing. But as people spent more time there and realised how important these places were to their livelihoods, the shacks began to improve. They became more like dorms. People who provided support services began to move in, like women who prepared the fishermen's food, washed their clothes, and suchlike. Thus the útver morphed into something called *votbúðir*, or "wet camps".

Over time, other dwellings began to be built near the votbúðir. These were cleaner and more comfortable than the tiny shacks that had previously housed the intrepid seafarers. These were called *þurrbúðir*, "dry camps".

Gradually, other establishments were set up near the votbúðir and þurrbúðir to service the fishermen and their operations even further. And that is how fishing villages were born.

23 Foremen's intuition

For centuries, people went out fishing in open rowboats. I'm sure I don't need to elaborate on the hazards involved. After all, we are talking about the North Atlantic, and weather conditions could change instantly.

Consequently, accidents at sea were far too common. Sometimes virtually all the men from a single district were wiped out in one disaster.

Those open rowboats generally had six to ten oars, meaning they were rowed by three or four people. I use "people" because even though those who went fishing were usually male, this wasn't always the case. Women also rowed, and in fact there are even one or two women known to have been foremen (or, well, *forewomen*) on fishing boats.

A foreman had a hugely important job. (I'll stick with the male pronoun because in Iceland women are men, as I explained in the first *Little Book*.) He was the captain of his vessel, charged with assessing conditions at any given time to determine whether it was safe to go out.

The foreman needed to be extremely attuned to nature and all her signals, and each formed his own particular way of interpreting these. Usually he would wake up in the night while everyone else was sleeping and go outside to check on conditions. If the moon was out, he might "read" the clouds. Their position and shape around nearby mountains and over the surface of the sea would determine where he and his crew rowed the following day, and how far out. If, for example, there was a mackerel sky (a cloud formation with ripples), it would likely mean that the day would be good and they could venture out further than if the clouds were different.

Or the foreman might wade out into the sea and listen to the wind. If there was a heavy tide, that would give him an indication of what the waves were like further out. Some foremen even tasted the water. Not sure how they made sense of their findings in that regard, but it was all a part of coming up with a unique system of interpretation.

Sometimes the foreman decided not to row out that day, and couldn't really explain why. Stories exist of boats setting off from a given location and one of the foremen having a "feeling" and deciding not to go - and later in the day a storm blowing in. Everyone perished except the crew of the boat with the foreman who had trusted his intuition. And so, a good and intuitive foreman was obviously someone you wanted to know, and with whom you wanted to row.

24 Seafaring superstitions

Fishing on the open seas was one of those activities that was fraught with risk and uncertainty. Consequently: superstitions, almost all of them aimed at keeping people safe while out at sea.

For instance there were these letters called *himnabréf*, "heaven letters", that Christ was supposed to have written and which provided instruction as to the correct form of behaviour and such. These were not unique to Iceland, but were known throughout Europe. Over time they somehow morphed into letters that, if carried on your person, would protect you from harm. Those were the letters folks carried on them when they went out to sea, in the hope that they would be spared from drowning.

Similar in nature were little hollow stones, called *aggarsteinar*. They floated, and if carried on you they were supposed to protect you from drowning. (And while I see the logic, I'm supposing a lot of those puppies would have been needed to actually keep you afloat).

Not all superstitions were about safety, though - some had more to do with prosperity. This included the *aflakló*, or "catch claw", a cut-off foot of a heron that a fisherman would keep in his shoe. He would then wait for it to prick the bottom of his foot. When it did, it was time to put out a net. Not sure how it worked if there was more than one fisherman with an aflakló in his shoe, and if they all pricked at different times. Maybe they just kept throwing out nets and consequently catching lots of fish, thereby fulfilling the prophecy.

Other superstitions were a bit more nebulous. For instance, some things were never supposed to be called by their real names while out at sea. Like a swordfish (Icelandic: *sverðfiskur*) was never supposed to be called that, but rather *vopnafiskur*, or "weapons fish". If called by its real name, it would bring bad luck.

The first fish caught in any fishing excursion was called a *Maríufiskur* - "Mary's fish" (indubitably a reference to the Virgin Mary and thus a throwback to Catholicism), and it was always supposed to be kept until the crew arrived back on land and then given to a poor widow. Even today the first salmon caught in any fishing excursion or angling season is called *Maríulax*, or "Mary's salmon", though I don't believe the poor-widow tradition exists any more.

Many of the seafaring superstitions were connected to women, who were supposed to bring very bad luck. Like if a fisherman passed a woman on his way out to the fishing station or to a boat, it was Bad News. If a fisherman dreamed about a woman before rowing out to sea, especially if he was in close contact with that woman, it was supposed to foreshadow bad weather. One foreman reportedly never went out fishing if he dreamed about his grandmother the night before, since the old lady was invariably highly agitated in his dream.

Finally - and I'll leave it to you to decide whether this constitutes superstition - the crew of a boat never rowed

out to sea until they had said a prayer together. The fishermen would climb into their boat, take off their hats, bow their heads, and pray. This was known as the *Sjómannabæn* (Seafarer's Prayer) and no one was permitted to go out unless they had learned it. There were several variations on the prayer, but essentially it went something like this:

Oh my Lord and my God, as I row out to fish and sense my powerlessness and the weakness of this vessel against the hidden forces of the air and water, I lift up to you my eyes of hope and faith, and ask you in Jesus' name to lead us safely to the open sea.

25 Bounty

Even when farmers didn't go out fishing (or before they had discovered what a fine prospect it could be), they soon discovered that living near the sea could be a Very Good Thing. So good, in fact, that the crown and the church were super quick to catch on, and made a point of usurping all the best land bordering the ocean.

As it happened, the sea yielded lots of great stuff besides fish. Like driftwood, for instance. Oh boy. In a country with hardly any wood, what a massive perk it was to get logs of driftwood delivered practically to your doorstep. And not just any wood. Wood from freaking Siberia. Wood that had circled the North Pole several times before it came to alight on Icelandic shores. Wood that, as a result, was remarkably tough - fortified by years of rolling around out at sea. Badass *survivor* wood.

Everybody wanted that wood. Which is why every farmer who had sea access was given a special mark that he scratched into the wooden logs to stake his claim to them. A mark that loudly and clearly proclaimed MINE, AND GET YER DIRTY HANDS OFF IT.

That's how important it was.

Second reason for wanting a seaside home, besides the view: all that kelp and seaweed. Somehow people discovered that the stuff was actually quite nutritious and that, in a pinch, sheep could be sent down to the shore to graze on it. ("Pinch" generally meaning that something had happened to your hay and your sheep were about to starve to death.) Also that seaweed could be fed to the cows, and could be mixed in with the hay to make it last longer.

Moreover, stuck to the seaweed were often mussels just begging to be eaten. Also, if your seashore had cliffs it would probably have birds, and those birds laid eggs, and those eggs were just there for the picking ... as long as you had nerves of steel and were prepared to rappel down the cliff face to fetch them. And even if you didn't filch the eggs and just let the birds have their nests and their chicks and everything, you could still collect down feathers from the nests when they were done and use it to make duvets and mattresses and pillows.

Then there were the seals. They lounged around on the shores and were an easy prey, especially in the *sellátur*, the place where they went to give birth to their

young. The seal hunters would go there, wait for the mummy and daddy seals to leave for the day, and then BAM! club the baby seals to death.

I know.

Very occasionally there would be huge amounts of fish that washed up on shore. For example in 1669, in a place called Staðasveit on the Snæfellsnes peninsula, several hundred dead catfish suddenly floated up on the coastline. Almost exactly a century later, in 1770, *four thousand* catfish washed up on the very same shore. And nobody knows why.

But the greatest, most fantastic bonus of all was the *hvalreki*. A literal translation of the term is impossible, though "washed-up whale" comes pretty close. As the name suggests, it was a beached whale. One of those beasts could feed an entire district in a single swoop, or could keep the household of a farm fed for a year. In fact a hvalreki was such an amazing stroke of luck that, to this day, the word is still used to denote a wind-fall. Like if something unexpected happens that means massive good fortune, you might say: *Þvílíkur hvalreki!* - "what a windfall", though literally translated it means: "What a beached whale!"

26 Indebted to the district

One of the darkest stains on Iceland's historical fabric has got to be the law that allowed district authorities to dissolve households when the male head of that household died.

It happened frequently. In a treacherous landscape with an unforgiving climate, death was everywhere. Men drowned at sea, got lost in fog, fell into crevices, became ill from malnourishment, or simply vanished.

When a man died, his widow would be left with the children and whatever farmhands were living at the farm. However, she was not permitted, by law, to continue farming on her own. Virtually before her husband's body was cold in the grave the authorities would arrive and auction off the land (if the farmer happened to own the land) and pretty much all possessions (the widow might be allowed to take a chest with her personal belongings; the children perhaps some of their toys). If the land happened to be very bountiful, or bordered the sea, those selfsame authorities might just make sure that the land went to them. Or the church would step in and claim it. Whatever it took to usurp the best land for those already in power.

When the land and all possessions had been auctioned off, the members of the household would be sent off to live at whatever farms would take them in. For money, of course. It was the duty of the district in which they lived to look after them (mind you, they had to have lived there at least ten years to qualify - which, given that the Icelanders were always on the move, was probably asking a lot), and their objective was to look after them in the cheapest way possible. Meaning they would farm the welfare cases-slash-dependents out to the lowest bidder.

Almost every family in Iceland has a story of an ancestor who was affected by such a household dissolution. In my family it was my grandmother. Her father, my great-grandfather, died, and my great-grandmother was left with four children. Even though she wanted to keep the farm and there was nothing physically preventing her from doing so, she was not allowed to. Instead the authorities showed up a few days later to begin the auction. The evening before, an official of the district reportedly came and advised her to hide her *sæng* - her duvet. Pretty much every Icelander alive has their very own sæng from the day they are born, and it becomes a very personal and intimate possession. The fact that the authorities were prepared to auction off her sæng speaks volume about the lack of sanctity for even the most private of possessions. Everything was taken.

My great-grandmother was sent away to become a labourer on a farm. She was permitted to take one of her children with her, but the other three were all sent out to separate farms. My grandmother was first fostered out to a farm where she was treated very badly. Later she was sent to another, where the people were kind. Those people effectively raised her, and she always spoke very fondly of them as her foster parents.

People who were sent out to farms in this manner were the *niðursetningar*. The literal translation of the word is "put downers", and it was very shameful to be a niðursetningur, even when you had done nothing to bring it on yourself. To exacerbate the injustice, the money that the district paid for your upkeep accumulated as a debt that you had to pay back. Obviously this gave the authorities vast control over your life (although the authorities had vast control over everybody's life, so that wasn't too much of a departure). If, for example, you wanted to marry, you were not allowed to if you had received what was somewhat erroneously dubbed *sveitastyrkur*, "district support", at some point in the previous ten years. That is, unless you could pay back the debt, which was hardly likely, especially if you were a woman, because where were you going to get the money? You had to work, sure, but you didn't get paid.

The convoluted thing in all this was that it was ostensibly done to reduce the number of district dependents. The common notion, at least as far as the law was concerned, was that a woman could not manage a farm on her own. She and her children would inevitably wind up destitute and have to be supported by the state. Which boggles the mind, because that's exactly what happened when those people were driven off their land and into the "care" of the district.

Which leads me to think that there might have been another, more sinister one, reason. For instance that the law was specifically designed to allow crown and church to seize land that had the potential to yield wealth, like land that bordered the sea.

27 Lamb in a barrel

Without question, the single most important animal in Iceland back in the day was the sheep. Without the sheep, the Icelandic people would have been extinct within a few years of settlement on their hostile, weather-beaten rock.

A wealthy man in the Iceland of old was a man who owned many sheep. Even today the Icelandic word *fé* means both "money" and "sheep", and the old word for "shepherd", *féhirðir*, is the word used for "treasurer" today.

It should come as no surprise, then, that lambing season was one of the most important, and delicate, times of year. Bringing those little lambs into the world and keeping them alive was a task that was not to be taken lightly.

But sometimes a lamb wouldn't make it. When that happened, the immediate problem was how to keep the ewe milking as long as possible, since ewes' milk was a staple of the Icelanders' diet. If a ewe lost her lamb, another lamb had to be found as its replacement.

This usually meant taking a lamb from a ewe that had one to spare, and parading that lamb in front of the bereaved ewe to try to get her to adopt it. This didn't always work, since it turns out that ewes are a bit particular and will not allow just any old lamb to suckle their precious teats. A strategy was required. This sometimes involved rubbing the liver of the lamb that had died on the head of the lamb that was supposed to be its replacement. If that didn't work, the hide of the dead lamb would be sewn onto the replacement lamb, after which it would be locked inside a shed with its intended foster mother. Ideally the ewe would be duped by this crafty plan and think that the lamb with the sewn-on hide was her own little lamb come back to life.

If all else failed, and the stubborn ewe refused to adopt the lamb, the changeling would be put inside a barrel where it would commence to bleat incessantly. The ewe would be tied up next to the barrel, or confined in a small space next to it. When the lamb was finally released, the ewe would ideally break down and gather the baby to its bosom. I suppose even the hardest-hearted ewes have trouble withstanding the pitiful bleating of a lamb in a barrel ... though of course it's possible she just wanted to *stop that bloody noise.*

On the other hand, if the situation was reversed - if the ewe died and the lamb lived - the first course of action was to try to get another ewe to adopt it. If that didn't work (see above), the orphaned lamb would usually be taken in by the farm folk. Such lambs were called *heimalningar,* "home raised", and tended to become the household darlings, since they invariably grew very attached to the farm people. This was especially true of the children, who were often charged with their feeding.

Each child on a farm was usually allowed to claim one lamb as their own during lambing season. They didn't exactly own the lambs, but could adopt them. The children would spend inordinate amounts of time cuddling their little lambs ... but they had to be careful not to kiss them, because if they did, superstition had it that it would get eaten by a fox when it was sent to the mountain pasture later that summer.

28 What the sheep gave

So we've established that sheep were important to the Icelanders' survival, but what exactly did they provide?

Answer: almost everything.

First, of course, the wool. Sheep were shorn near the beginning of June, by which time the wool was so long that it was literally hanging off them and could be removed by hand. That's right: shears didn't actually come into play until the 19th century. (So I guess "shorn" isn't the correct term, strictly speaking. "Handed" is probably more accurate.)

In any case, when the wool was off, it was washed in warm urine that was kept gently simmering over a fire. (No I am not making this up). After that it was rinsed (thoroughly, we hope) in a brook or river, before being laid out to dry.

The wool was then carded, spun, and knitted into sweaters, socks, hats, underwear, mittens, trousers, blankets and just about anything else that could conceivably be used to cover a human body.

Meanwhile, the pelt of the sheep was used for outerwear (picture hip and cool sheepskin vest) and for shoes (picture tragically unhip, slipper-like thingies).

The meat, obviously, was eaten. Sometimes fresh, although fresh wasn't all that appealing to the old Icelandic palate. Folks were used to meat being preserved in some way, like salted or smoked, so that's what they preferred. Naturally the offal was eaten, too. Hell, anything that *could* be eaten, was eaten. Even the blood, which was mixed with fat and grain or Iceland moss, and made into pudding. The lungs, liver and heart were boiled and eaten fresh or pickled. The glands (pardon me: the *sweetbreads*) were imbibed, too. The colon was either chopped up and mixed into the blood pudding concoction, or stuffed with meat and pickled. The heads and feet were singed (burned) to remove all the hairs, kept until they started to go rancid (this was supposed to enhance the flavour), then ingested. Either that or they were boiled before they reached their rancid state, and then pickled. The brain was boiled, mashed with salt, and eaten - or kneaded with grain and made into cakes that were boiled and eaten as an accompaniment to the singed sheep's heads and feet. The testicles of the ram were boiled and pickled, to be consumed at a later date.

Incidentally, nearly all of the above (ahem) *delicacies* are available today at your local Icelandic supermarket, though many of them are seasonal. The only exceptions I believe are the lungs, colon, sweetbreads, brain and feet - I've never encountered those in a grocery store, though I can't rule out that they are sold somewhere.

The sheep had some interesting medical uses, as well. For example, the lungs were sometimes fried up and consumed on an empty stomach "as an antidote to an alcoholic drink", according to *Íslenzkir þjóðhættir*.

In layman's terms this means: "To help you get wasted without suffering a massive hangover the next day." The singed meat of a ram was supposed to cure a facial rash, ram's fat was supposed to be good for burns, ram piss mixed with honey was supposed to alleviate oedema, and ash from burned sheep's bones was believed to be good for healing cuts and burns.

Furthermore, burning a ram's horn was supposed to be good for keeping ghosts away (always handy).

Last, but definitely not least, the bones of the sheep were toys for children. The joints were sheep, the jawbones cows (the teeth were the udders), and the shin bones horses. These toys were called "children's gold" and were invariably highly treasured by their owners.

29 Leadership. I mean sheep.

In spite of their extensive dependence on sheep, the Icelanders have long considered them rather stupid animals. Like if you really want to insult someone, you might call them *sauðheimskur*, which literally means "sheep stupid". Or if you want to describe someone as being uncouth, you'd say *hann er algjör sauður*, meaning "he's a total sheep".

Which is why it's ironic that a type of sheep exists

that is apparently unique to the Icelandic sheep breed: the *forystukind*, or "leader sheep". (Actually, "leadership sheep" if you want to get technical, but that sounds a little convoluted.)

These leader sheep - who are frequently rams, but not always - somehow conclude that they are the leaders of a flock. To be the owner of a leader sheep in the old days was a Very Good Thing (and it still is, though perhaps marginally less important than it was back then). The leader sheep seemed to have a sixth sense about the best place to tread, which was a highly useful thing in the winter. After all, snow could easily be covering deep cracks or crevices that you sure as hell wouldn't want to tumble into if you were a sheep - or anybody for that matter. Somehow the leader sheep instinctively knew where the snow was shallowest and therefore where it was best to tread, even if the ground wasn't visible.

Leader sheep had a built-in compass that guided them home in blizzards, fog, or darkness. Many a leader sheep has saved the lives of both its flock and the shepherd, who no doubt quickly realised that following where the leader sheep led was a very good idea. For instance if the leader sheep showed clear signs of wanting to leave the pasture and go home, the shepherd would almost always comply. Sure enough: a blizzard would usually blow in soon afterward. The leader sheep generally slept near the door of the sheep shed, but when it moved away from the door and further into the shed the shepherd could usually take it as a sign that a storm was gathering, of the kind that was not safe for sheep (or anyone) to be out in.

So obviously a leader sheep was a pretty amazing creature, and far from being "sheep stupid". And naturally they were highly valued. When their less clairvoyant brethren were sent to the slaughter, the leader sheep generally remained at home, coddled and catered to, very often living to the ripe old age of thirteen or fourteen. And if at some point during their lives they were sold, their owners were always able to fetch a handsome price for them.

30 Food glorious food

It is pretty easy to scoff at all the putrid food the Icelanders imbibed in the old days. But before we do, let us take a moment to remember that, when it came to food, the Iceland of old was no different from any other place in the world. People's lives have always revolved around food: how to get it, how to cook it, and how to conserve it. And in Iceland, given the hardly-any-firewood problem, finding the best way to preserve and prepare food using a minimal amount of energy was paramount.

Take the perennially popular putrid shark. Today we think of it largely as a joke - give tourists a small piece of "cured shark" (snicker) and watch their faces twist in abject horror before they start shouting bloody murder at being tricked into imbibing something so heinous.

But here's the thing: this particular shark (the Greenland shark) is of a species that stores urine in its flesh

(I know, *delightful*). You may want to think of it as ammonia, because that's basically what it is. Now, if you ingested this ammonia in the old days you would likely die a horrible death. That shark needed to go through some serious detoxification before it was fit for human consumption. To that end it was buried in the ground for several weeks to allow the ammonia to seep out of it, and then hung out to dry. By which time it had developed a rather, shall we say, *pungent* flavour. Yet it fulfilled its purpose - providing nourishment to people without sending them to their graves in the process.

Also: hanging meat up over a fire, preferably if the firewood was dung (the best seasoning they had at the time), was a conservation method par excellence. Pickling: also highly popular. For that they used the whey from the skyr, which was the most common dairy product in the Iceland of old, next to plain milk. After you made your skyr (a curdling agent was put into the milk, taken from the stomach of a calf that had been slaughtered, and it made the milk curdle and thus you got your skyr, *yes I know*) you were left with this barrel of whey into which you could basically dump any and all meat or fish, and it would be preserved. As a bonus, the whey was rich in vitamins and protein, so you could drink it - though it tasted pretty abominable, at least to the modern palate. It is very sour and can last for ages without going bad ... indeed, back then people considered whey to be at its best when it was around two years old, by which time they probably considered it to have aged properly. Incidentally, you can still buy it in the store if you so desire (and I do not know why you would, except maybe to use as a poor substitute for white wine in recipes).

Last, but not least, there was the drying method (always a crowd-pleaser), which was used for fish in particular. Dried fish was a staple of the Icelanders' diet, and we still enjoy it today, though we don't normally eat it as a full meal - more as a snack, with butter on top. Back in the day, however, it constituted the main meal of the day, which was usually eaten around two or three in the afternoon. Dried fish, which we call *harðfiskur*, or "hard fish", is another food that tourists tend to turn up their noses at because they think it stinks. Icelanders, on the other hand, seem incapable of finding anything wrong with the smell of dried fish - differing, in that respect, from just about every other species of human.

31 Ration

It would be a gross aberration to say that the Icelanders of old ate a diversified diet. There was dairy and there were animal proteins, and maybe, if people were lucky, there might a handful of grain. That was about it.

The main meals of the day were breakfast, which was eaten around six am (which they called *miðmorgun* - "mid-morning" ... go figure), a lunch of sorts, eaten around ten or eleven am, and then the main meal of the day, eaten around two or three pm. None of the sources

I consulted made mention of a later meal, which is odd. I find it hard to believe that people received no nourishment between three and ten pm, when the kvöldvaka ended. But what do I know? Maybe they were really into fasting back then.

The first two meals usually consisted of skyr and milk. Failing that, there was some kind of gruel, plus milk. Curiously, both of these meals were called *skattur*, which today is the word for tax. The earlier meal was called *litli-skattur* - "little tax", and the second one was just ... skattur.

The midday meal usually consisted of dried fish and butter - a major staple in the Icelanders' diet, as I said - and occasionally a meat or fish soup, or a milky gruel.

Butter was highly coveted in those days, and was often used as currency. Farmhands would get paid in butter, and would trade it for things that they needed or wanted. Rent for land or livestock was also sometimes paid in butter, so wealthy landowners often wound up with mountains of the stuff. Butter was almost always unsalted, so it might have tasted a little bland - but of course the resourceful Icelanders had a remedy for that: let it go sour. This (ahem) enhanced the flavour, and also acted as a preservative. In fact you could keep your butter supplies intact for around two years by using this ingenious method.

But why this obsession with butter? Well, it was highly coveted because butter is around eighty percent fat, and back in the day, *fat was good*. Counting calories was not their main concern back then - at least not the way we do it today. Nowadays we try to keep the count low.

Back then, they tried to keep it high. And fatty foods were in great demand in a country where high-calorie fare was not readily available, but where tons of energy was required just to cope with the daily business of living.

On large farms where many people lived, each worker would receive a certain amount of fish and butter with which they would have to make do for an entire week. In other words, they had to make it last. None of this wolfing down your ration on the first day, unless you wanted to starve for the next six or so. And naturally the women got shafted. Typically a man would receive five kilograms of dried fish for the week, and 1.75 kg of butter. Female workers got about a quarter of that amount. Sure, the menfolk probably did a bit more heavy lifting, but even so. I'm sure the women had to do plenty of work that required serious exertion.

So the women got the short end of the stick in this regard, though with one notable exception: the mistress of the house got to dole out the rations. Hers was the power to feed or starve. If she liked you, she might slip you a little extra. If she did not ... well, let's just say that being on her bad side was not a situation that anybody relished.

32 Grains and subs

Food in Iceland was not always as dreadfully scarce as it would later become. When the first settlers arrived, not only did they find plenty of forest, they were also able to grow wheat and other grains. Then, as we know, forests were chopped down, mini-ice age came, there was no more firewood, people had to stop taking saunas, everyone moved in together, got lice, and proceeded to starve.

By 1550, wheat flour was a commodity virtually unheard of in Iceland. When the populace did manage to get a hold of some, it came via the Danish overlords and was usually infested with maggots or similar delights. Not to mention that it was ridiculously expensive. And if people disliked the goods, they couldn't just skip off to the other flour seller down the road. There wasn't one. The Danes had a monopoly. They called the shots.

Because it was so precious, the Nicelanders came up with ways of making their flour last. They mixed it with dried seaweed, or moss, or both. (Aside: this moss of which I speak - called *fjallagrös* - is not of the squishy green or grey variety that you see all over Iceland, but is generally quite hard and dry and chew-able, with a decidedly bitter taste. In later years it has been found to have all these healing properties that no one had had any idea about in the old days. So in fact the Icelanders were imbibing something highly nutritious when they thought they were just eating the equivalent of dried cardboard in order to survive. Talk about a hvalreki!)

Naturally this dearth of grain meant that bread and other flour-based comestibles were a major luxury. Which is why they came up with *laufabrauð* - "leaf bread". Laufabrauð are very thin, round pieces of bread ... so thin, in fact, that they hardly deserve to be called "bread". They're more like tortillas, only the laufabrauð are decorated with pretty cut-out designs and then deep-fried until crispy. Akin to Indian papadums, perhaps, only without the spices (and prettier).

Today laufabrauð are a cherished delicacy at Christmas and are normally eaten with the traditional *hangikjöt*, or smoked lamb. Indeed, some families have a long-standing tradition whereby they gather together in the lead-up to Christmas to make laufabrauð (whereas the rest of us just fetch them from the supermarket).

This thriftiness in the grain department is also how the ubiquitous *flatkökur* - "flat cakes" - came into being. As the name suggests these are flat, round cakes (though in the packages you buy nowadays they're usually cut in two so they're shaped like half-moons), made of rye and cooked on a skillet until they're slightly burnt. You can even buy them with Iceland moss, for an extra dose of nutrition. (Tip: don't buy them unless they're made the same day, preferably if they're still warm in the packet. Eat with butter and hangikjöt for best results.)

Last but not least there are the beloved Icelandic pancakes, or *pönnukökur*. These are more like French crêpes than American pancakes, for the reasons stated above. They are usually sprinkled with sugar before being rolled up and served, or spread with jam and whipped cream before being folded over twice. Their popularity has not waned over the centuries, and I don't believe an Icelander exists who doesn't love them. Apart from their deliciousness, they are somehow intricately tied up with our national identity. Plus, most of us associate them with happy times in our lives. Pönnukökur, you see, still tend to be made when there is something to celebrate.

33 The absent food group

There was one food group notoriously absent in the Iceland of yore: fruits and vegetables. And with good reason: there were precious few vegetables available in the old days, and no fruits. None. Not even imported fruits, because ... well, I'm sure you can guess. By the time they travelled all the way to Iceland from more temperate climes they were a squishy, repulsive mess.

Even in my early childhood in the 1960s, fruit was pretty scarce. The only fruit I remember seeing were bananas, oranges and apples. Red apples. Yellow apples, which the Icelanders always called green apples, came later. They were pretty expensive, and boy, were they a treat. If you wanted to offer someone something really good, you'd offer them a green apple.

So with this absence of fruits and veggies, how did the Icelanders manage to keep the doctor away?

Partly with the aforementioned Iceland moss. That, and the seaweed. Plus, there is this plant called scurvy-wort that grows all over the country and has loads of vitamin C. As the name implies, it helps fight scurvy, and played a huge role in maintaining the health of the Icelanders of old. In fact it is probably the main reason why the Icelanders had such good teeth until sugar, the scourge of dental hygiene anywhere, came to the country.

So yeah, basically the Icelandic people survived by eating grass.

And evidently that sufficed. Because even after the Icelanders were introduced to potatoes, which you'd think would be *eagerly* embraced for their nutritional value, they were slow to change their ways. Like with the oil lamps, they were dismissive of this newfangled produce. Growing potatoes took up too much space. Space that could be used to make hay. Finally a campaign was launched in the 17th century extolling the virtues of the humble potato, and the Icelanders - always receptive to the forces of marketing - began to come around. They haven't looked back since.

34 Annihilation of the pearly whites

So yes, the Icelanders preserved their pearly whites re-markably well. We know this because human skulls have been excavated from way, way back, and they still have the teeth very much intact. Granted, their owners might never have scored a Colgate commercial, but their teeth were able to get the masticating done, and done well.

And then came the evil substance SUGAR. The Ice-landic populace fell for it hook, line and sinker. Sugar quickly became *the* indispensable commodity, right up there with coffee, tobacco and a nip of Brennivín (Ice-landic liquor, colloqually referred to as Black Death).

And like most vices, sugar left a trail of destruction in its wake. For the first time, the natives came to know the agony of dental decay and diseased gums.

This called for creative remedies to help numb the pain. One favoured method was to break off the tooth of a mouse and stick it into the gum next to the offend-ing tooth. Another was to place the faeces of a year-old male child in the same spot. (I gather the feces of fe-male children didn't have the same healing properties.) Or placing the tooth of a dead man next to the decayed tooth. Or pulverising the teeth of a dog, and ingesting the powder. (I'm guessing there were a lot of toothless dogs around.) Then, if all else failed, you could always remove the aching tooth and make your own implant us-ing the tooth of a corpse. (No, I am not making this up.)

Anything but go on a sugar-free diet. In fact anyone suggesting such an atrocity would probably have been banished to the highlands, stat.

35 Precious salt

That was sugar. Now let's talk a little about salt.

Today we have an oversupply of the stuff. Much of our food is saturated with it, whether we like it or not. But back in the Iceland of old it was both scarce and highly coveted. Very little salt was imported, and when it was it was out of the price range of ordinary folk, except in very limited quantities.

So what did people do when they had no salt?

Well, you might think (as I did) that their first course of action would be to make some. After all, they had an abundance of salty water all around the country ... couldn't they just boil the hell out of the sea until there was plenty of salt left over?

Well, yes they could. In theory. Except that boiling like hell requires a big fire, and a big fire requires lots of firewood. You see where I'm going with this, right?

Yep. I'm going nowhere.

Not to be undone, the Icelanders adopted a different strategy: freezing the sea water. They would take it, leave it to freeze, scrape the ice off the top, thaw it, freeze it again, scrape the ice off the top ... until eventually, like maybe ten years down the road, they had about a half a cup of salt to show for their efforts. And who the hell wants to wait that long to put salt on their food? Not me - and not the Icelanders. Which is why they ended by taking some seaweed, drying it, burning it, and then sprinkling the ash on their dinner.

So the next time you grind some of that premium coarse sea salt onto your filet mignon with your fancy salt dispenser, spare a thought for the poor Icelanders. With grey ash all over their food.

36 Beggars and vagabonds

In spite of their valiant efforts to impose social order, the Icelandic authorities were not entirely successful in eliminating vagabonds. At any given time in Iceland's history there was a significant number of people roaming from farm to farm, managing to procure free food and lodgings for themselves.

Some of them were folks that had obtained permission to be freelancers. You'll recall that they hired themselves out to different farms, usually during haymaking season. But as with all freelancers there were times when the work dried up, when they were, as they say, "between jobs". At such times they sometimes morphed into travelling salespeople, touring the country on foot and peddling whatever wares they managed to carry on their person. Things like linen, needles, knives, scissors and the ever-coveted books, to name but a few.

That was one group of vagabonds. Others ... well, they were often folks who just didn't feel like working.

They pretended to be on Very Important Business, moving from one farm to the next en route to the place where their VIB was supposed to be conducted. And the Icelanders, hospitable by nature, rarely turned these weary travellers away. Some folks could keep going like that indefinitely ... or at least until the jig was up and farmers realised that they and their hospitality had been taken for a ride.

But some vagabonds were truly tragic cases. They simply had no choice but to drift around. Iceland had no hospital back in the day, and when King Christian III of Denmark (and Iceland) was asked in the 16th century to build one for his poor downtrodden Icelandic subjects he refused, declaring that physically or mentally ill persons would have to depend on the kindness of strangers. In other words: become drifters. They were thereby given official permission to be vagabonds, and were called *kóngsins flækingar* or "the king's vagrants". A dastardly predicament, particularly when times were rough, like after the Skaftáreldar eruption in the 18th century that caused widespread famine and wiped out a large share of the population. At such times the ill and infirm competed not only with other sick people for food and lodgings, but with able-bodied folks as well. Trails between farms were often strewn with corpses at that time, of sick and starving people who had been turned away repeatedly and simply collapsed.

Some vagrants weren't sick, though - they were just outcasts thought of as "odd". Either that or they were "difficult" - perhaps with some unfortunate flaws of character. No one wanted to offer someone like that a

permanent position at their farm, so there was nothing for such unfortunates to do but to drift. Also, when
times were hard farms simply did not produce enough
to feed those who already lived there, so taking in ad-
ditional people was out of the question - even if they
seemed perfectly healthy and normal. Consequently
people who in more favourable years might have found
a position, would in bad years have been forced to drift.

These poor outcasts would often try to cultivate some skill or routine with which to entertain people, since this improved their chances of being sheltered and fed. Some of them were very well informed about particular subjects (they might be diagnosed with Aspergers or autism today), and were welcome guests for that reason. Others sang, or sketched, or composed and recited poetry (the rappers of yonder days). Or whatever.

So vagabonds were hardly ever turned away when they came to a farm, except when times were exceptionally tough. They would always be given food and shelter for a night or two, at least. Sometimes more than one arrived at one time, though, and this could spell trouble. Apparently vagabonds were renowned for their animosity towards each other, since they looked upon others in the same situation as rivals. The jibes and insults could fly something awful, usually to the great amusement of the farm folk.

Some vagrants made a point of being useful by doing chores or menial jobs. Others were lazy and wanted only to be put up for free. Unsurprisingly those of the latter ilk were pretty unpopular, but they were tolerated (no doubt with a gnashing of teeth) because they could be spiteful and spread gossip. And if there was one thing the farm folk dreaded even more than a lazy vagabond, it was to have gossip spread about their alleged inhospitality. Clearly, then, vagabonds held a fair bit of power in the Iceland of old, more than they probably realised.

37 Aliens in Iceland

It is easy to think of the Iceland of yore as a barren rock in the North Atlantic that never saw any action from abroad, except when the king sent his minions over to impose some law or other on the poor, snivelling Icelanders.

Not so. Foreigners came and went on a regular basis. Ships from the European continent, especially England and France, routinely fished off the Icelandic coast and thus their crews often came ashore - though not always willingly. Sometimes they washed up on shore after their ships went down - dead, alive, or in various stages in between.

On the whole, the Icelandic populace appears to have been reasonably welcoming to foreign visitors. After all, the Icelanders were a hospitable people, who dreaded being called uncongenial. But alas, they did not always live up to their personal best in such matters. Just ask the poor Basque sailors who washed up on the West Fjords after their ship was wrecked in a storm. Obviously they were not able to return home by the same means as they came, and so found themselves lost in a hostile landscape with no way to fend for themselves. They went and knocked on doors, and some people took pity on them and put them up for a couple of nights. But that was not a long-term solution, and eventually they found that all doors had been shut. Consequently they resorted to desperate measures: breaking into places and stealing food and other essentials. When the district magistrate, the formidable Ari í Ögri, found out, he sent a posse of his best men to search for them, and ordered that they should all be executed. Which they duly were. This shameful event in Iceland's history has since been dubbed *Spánarvígin*, or "the Spanish killings".

I'm tempted to blame this on the fact that West Fjords folk were a little, um, paranoid. They travelled to some pretty dark places, metaphysically speaking. For instance, someone would get it into their head that someone else was causing some third person grief (sickness, misfortune, or whatever), and before you could say *voodooforyou* they'd be accusing them of witchcraft and burning them at the stake. It was Iceland's version of the witch hunts.

Meanwhile, the East Icelanders - people who lived on the East Fjords - were as blithe and sunny as their western counterparts were dark and morose. They were open and tolerant and embraced foreigners. And how! In fact there is a strain of Icelander with dark hair and brown eyes that bears testimony to how well the East Fjords folk embraced French sailors that regularly fished off the coast of East Iceland.

This was also the home of one Hans Jónatan, the son of a Danish aristocrat and a Caribbean slave who became somewhat of a legend in the East. Hans Jónatan had had a pretty remarkable life before he alighted on Icelandic shores. Years earlier, his father, who had been a colonial governor in the southern seas, had brought his female slave and their young son (Hans Jónatan) back to Denmark with him. Amazingly this did not sit too well with his Danish wife, so when the governor died, she arranged for Hans Jónatan, who by then was an adolescent, to be shipped off to a plantation in the West Indies where he was to be a slave. But lo! Just before he was to sail Hans Jónatan disappeared, later turning up as a shop clerk in Djúpivogur, where a Dane who knew of his history recognised him. With his dark skin, Hans Jónatan stuck out like a sore thumb - but no one in Djúpivogur seemed to mind. He was well liked by his neighbours and eventually married an Icelandic woman with whom he had two children, and from whom there are many descendants.

38 A visitor comes to the farm

We've talked a little bit about how people went from farm to farm, and how they were hospitably received, except when they weren't. And how generally the coming of a visitor was a welcome thing, a celebrated thing, because, you know, there wasn't a heck of a lot happening in the rural outbacks of Iceland at the time, and a visitor would inevitably bring news, or gossip, or even just some new vibes.

As we know, guests were not only a welcome diversion,

but also a convenient way to get the word out about your own general excellence in the hospitality department. And to be properly hospitable and properly excellent, you had to be prepared for the visitor's arrival. Obviously the folks of old did not have the benefit of our modern devices to receive word of imminent visits, so they had to find other ways to foresee the arrival of a guest.

For instance someone might start yawning, or feeling a little queasy in the stomach, or might have an irresistible urge to sleep so that they just could not keep their eyes open. All of this signalled the arrival of a visitor.

If the cat began to lick its butt with its leg sticking straight up in the air it meant that a visitor was coming. The same applied if a dog lay on the floor with its front legs straight out and its head resting on them. If the nose pointed to the right, it meant that the visitor was a good person, but if the nose pointed to the left, it meant that the visitor was an unpleasant person.

If a fly buzzed incessantly around the baðstofa it boded the arrival of a visitor, and if that fly accosted one person in particular the visitor would be coming to see that person. Also, if the kettle made a certain buzzing sound when water was being boiled for coffee, it meant that a visitor was about to arrive.

As soon as someone noticed one of those portentous signs they'd grab a broom and start sweeping the floor. Then, when the much-anticipated guest *did* arrive, a specific set of procedures would kick in.

39 Godding on the window

If it was still daylight outside, the visitor would knock three times at the front door, or on the paneling at the front of the house. Three was the magic number. Three represented the holy trinity, and if there were *not* three knocks then you'd better not answer the door because the visitor was probably a ghost.

Having heard three knocks, the farmer or his wife would go to the door. The visitor would greet the host with a kiss on the mouth and say: *Sæll vertu* (or *sæl vertu* if it was a woman), which basically translates as "be happy" (yes it's true). This is still the common greeting today, though the more-or-less universal *hæ* ("hi") is hot on its heels in popularity ... if it hasn't surpassed it already.

The host would then respond: *Komdu sæll/sæl*, which means "come happy" and is also still the common greeting today.

If the visitor was someone the person knew well, or if the occasion was special, the greeting might be slightly more eloquent, such as: *Komdu sæll og blessaður*, meaning "come happy and blessed" (... and still commonly used today). This would be accompanied by a handshake *and* a kiss, to which yet another kiss would be added, along with the phrase: *Þakka þér fyrir síðast*, meaning "thank you for the last time [we met]". This, too, is used today - most Icelanders will say *takk fyrir síðast*, especially if they had a particularly enjoyable time with someone the last time they got together. Sometimes, and here I quote from *Íslenzkir þjóðhættir*, "... people took off their hat or headdress with their left hand, whipped their hair from their forehead with a little toss of the head, and kissed".

Incidentally, the above applied *only* if the visitor arrived during daylight hours. If that same visitor arrived after dark (which was practically every hour of the day in mid-winter) he or she needed to go to the window rather than knock on the door, because - as everyone knew - only ghosts knocked on the door after dark. When the person got to the window they would say: *Hér sé guð* - "here be God". (For some reason someone muttering at the window was considered less creepy than someone knocking at the door.) The people inside would then respond: *Guð blessi þig* - "God bless you", after which someone would go to the door to admit the visitor. This prescribed action at the window was called, prosaically enough, *að guða á glugga*, or "to God on the window". And that is probably the only time in the history of the world that God has been made into a verb.

40 Come happy, go happy, eat happy

So now that the visitor had safely arrived (and proven himself to be of the mortal rather than the spectral variety), the big question was: what to do with him?

Well, after all the kissing and blessing and tossing of the head on the front step, the visitor was taken by the hand (literally) and led through the farm tunnel into the baðstofa. There he first greeted everyone verbally, then moved around and kissed everyone. Having thus smooched his way around the room he would be invited to sit down and subsequently be made to recite any news he had. Again, these sorts of visits were pretty much the only transmission of news and gossip in those days - they were CNN and *Hello!* magazine all rolled into one, with a dash of *The Hidden People Chronicle* thrown in for good measure.

Now, if the visitor's clothes were wet (surely not an uncommon occurrence), one or more of the women would remove his wet clothing, wash his feet with warm water, and then bring him dry clothes to put on. (And people wonder why vagabonds chose to be vagabonds.)

Next they would bring food. And if the visitor had

any sense of protocol at all, he would eat it. It was considered inexcusably rude not to accept the food offered to you. But! The visitor must not appear greedy. Always, he should say: "You really shouldn't have - this was *completely* unnecessary", or something similar, irrespective of whether or not he meant it. Next he would need to cross himself and say "God reward you for this food" or something like that, to which the home folk would reply, "God bless you". After that they would all watch as he tucked into his grub - but God forbid that he should finish it! That was considered the epitome of rudeness, because by not clearing your plate you were, in effect, telling your hosts: "You have provided *such* an abundance of food that I can't *possibly* finish it. Your generosity overwhelms me".

After he had eaten, the visitor would sit for a while before getting up and thanking his hosts for the meal by kissing them on the lips. He would usually sit for a while before making as if to leave, then kiss everyone in the room goodbye, and the hostess twice - once as a farewell gesture, and once to thank her (again) for the food. The man of the house would then get up and accompany the departing guest through the tunnel to the front door. It was *absolutely essential* to accompany him to the door because, if this was not done, he would take all the sanity from the house. (This is still customary today, though I think it has been determined that the residents won't automatically go insane if someone forgets. It is simply considered polite, and references to the old days are made in jest, as in: "I'll walk you to the door so you don't take all the sanity with you, haha".)

At the door, an elaborate farewell ritual took place, similar to the greeting conventions described earlier. The visitor would bid farewell to the host with two or three kisses. Before each kiss, he would speak these words, or a variation thereof: *Vertu nú blessaður og sæll* - "be now blessed and happy", *þakka þér kærlega fyrir mig* - "thank you most kindly for what you have provided", and *feginn vil ég eiga þig að* - "it would be my fortune to have you as a friend". (Translations are approximate - unfortunately you can't convey the delightful nuances of this exactly.)

After that, the visitor would trot (or amble) off into the sunset.

Mind you, sometimes the visitor would not leave, but would stay the night. When he did, he was usually made to sleep in a bed with someone in the baðstofa. If the visitor was a Very Important Personage, and if the farm was so luxuriously equipped as to have a spare room (like a separate living room for receiving guests), he would be given the choice of sleeping there if he wanted. Still, he was always given the option of having someone sleep with him, just in case he was afraid of the dark.

41 Offensive sex

Which brings us to the prickly subject of sex.

Come. You must have wondered about it. All this talk about the baðstofa and no privacy, then on the other hand women who were preggers and having babies ... it just begs the question: *How the heck did they get it on back then?*

Sadly, I'm afraid I can't tell you. Not a lot of documentation exists about this stuff. Those scribble-happy Icelanders, who wrote chronicles of kings and gods in their own little corner of the baðstofa and recorded all sorts of things in their journals, from monumental historical events to the state of the weather, completely neglected to tell us about their sex lives.

It was very remiss of them.

What we do know, however, is that both church and king went to extreme lengths to curb the hanky panky. Any sort of sexual deviation was severely punished - "deviation" in this case meaning anything beyond the missionary position. The penal (no pun intended) code at the time was the so-called Stóridómur (English: The Grand Judgment), a set of laws written by a bunch of prudish males and adopted in 1564. The stated purpose of Stóridómur was to "reduce instances of sexual depravity", the most serious of which was incest in its various constellations. The law listed seventeen female relatives that men were not permitted to sleep with: mother, sister, daughter, stepmother, daughter-in-law, etcetera. (Am guessing that nothing remotely akin to homosexuality or bestiality ever entered the minds of those twenty-four founding fathers of Stóridómur.)

Folks found guilty of incest either had their heads cut off (men) or were tossed into an icy pool of water where spectators could gather for a picnic and watch them drown (women). That very pool still exists at Þingvellir, right at the end of the rift most people walk along when they visit, and it is still called Drekkingarhylur, or "Drowning Pool".

A slightly less heinous sexual offence was the ubiquitous practice of having children out of wedlock. For that, one or both parents had to pay a fine, the amount of which rose with each repeated instance. And lest you think they would just go on indefinitely in this manner, think again: after the fourth time they were made to choose between being flogged or ... (wait for it) ... *marrying each other*.

Indeed, old Stóridómur was no lamb to play with (Icelandic idiom). It even went so far as to permit the castration of vagrants against their will and without any sort of legal recourse, even if said vagrant died during the, um, operation. This was deemed necessary so they would not go around impregnating farmers' young daughters. Although given the description of most vagabonds, I would guess that a) having sex was the furthest thing from their minds, and b) farmers' daughters would avoid them like the plague.

Not that all those laws and regulations were confined

to unmarried or incestuous folks. Even the legally married were not exempt from the pious meddling of the church. For example, couples were forbidden to have sex the night before a holy day, or the night before a Friday, or for a full seven days before taking communion. A man was not allowed to take communion at all if he had ejaculated the night before, was not allowed to have sex with his wife during pregnancy, and not for forty days after she gave birth. Which by my calculations constitutes a period of about ten full months. (I'll leave you to ponder that at your leisure.)

Mind you, the above refers to the Catholic church, which reigned supreme in Iceland before the reformation in the mid-16th century. Not that the reformation changed much, mind, since Stóridómur was established soon afterwards and continued to impose its strict authoritarian rules on the Icelanders' sexual conduct.

42 Blue verses

I know I said that no one was writing about sex in the old days, and I fear I'll have to eat my words because it turns out that at least one person was. There exists one (count 'em) slightly racy manuscript that has been preserved from the old days. It is is called *The Saga of Bósi and Herraud* and dates back to the 15th century. And because people probably would have had some vital body part forcibly amputated had they been caught writing porn, it's all penned in this adorable allegorical language. To wit:

> "What is your business here?" she asked.
> "To let my foal drink from your wine spring," he said.
> "But can he, my man?" she said. "He will not be familiar with the sort of well house that I possess."
> "I shall lead him forth," he said, "and forcibly submerge him if he will not drink by other means."
> "Where is your foal, my heartfelt friend?" she said.
> "Between my legs," he replied, "and touch him now, but gently, for he is very skittish."

In his book *Landmarks of a Lifetime*, folkways scholar Árni Björnsson speculates that there was no shortage of lewd stories and verses back in the day, but that very few were ever written down. Possibly because they weren't considered worthy of the paper (or vellum) required to preserve them, but also because of the fear of the church and its mighty wrath.

Before we move on I have one more random factoid on the lewdness front. There were these cairns up in the highlands called *beinakerlingar* (bone crones), which in part referred to the large number of bones (animal bones, that is - horse bones in particular) that were commonly stuck into them. No definitive explanation for this odd custom exists, but it is believed that initially people wanted to let others know of their travels on eldom-traversed mountain trails, or inform them about wayward sheep. Consequently they scribbled notes and stuck them into the bones, which they then stuck into the cairns.

For some strange reason, this innocent and helpful practice turned into a habit of people writing racy verses and sticking those into the bones. They usually took the form of a verse written in the voice of a woman and addressed to the next traveller, urging him to prove his masculinity. These verses became known as *beinakerlinga-vísur* (bone crone verses), and over time the definition expanded to incorporate all lewd verses, which became collectively known under that name.

43 Fun fun fun

You may have the idea that life in the Iceland of old was little more than a dreary slog through endless days of back-breaking work, putrid food and miserable living conditions, alleviated only by the occasional fantasy of being carried off by a hidden person, or a lewd verse stuck into a bone.

But oh, how wrong you would be. Because the Icelanders also knew how to have fun. Yes they did.

How, you ask?

Well, for example they danced. They had this dance called Vikivaki where they all got in a circle, joined hands or clapped shoulders, and then did two steps to the left and one step to the right, occasionally changing rhythm, all to the sound of somebody chanting.

I know. Sounds like a blast. Which is just what the bishop at the time thought. In fact, he thought it sounded like a little *too much* of a blast. And it wasn't just the dancing, it was all the sordid decadence that went along with it. Apparently when folks got together to dance it loosened up their morals and allowed them to get carried off by their carnal urges. And then nine months later *hellooo baby*.

So the bishop came up with a crafty plan to take care the problem: make dancing illegal. (This was in the 12th century, if that tells you anything.)

But you know those impudent Icelanders. They never do as they're told. They just kept doing their two-steps-to-the-left, one-step-to-the-right, until in the 17th century the bishop had a minor conniption, banged his proverbial fist on the table, and declared that dancing was now absolutely, unequivocally banned and would not under any circumstances be tolerated because of all the bastards that were born afterwards. (This was obviously a different bishop, though.)

And to drive the point home, the Danish king sent one of his minions over to Iceland to ensure that them dancing and chanting infidels back in not-so-Niceland knew he meant business.

And clearly it worked, because from that point and for the next three hundred years or so, the Icelanders *did not dance*. (They kept having bastards, though.)

So does that mean they had no fun? No it does not.

They merely did other things to amuse themselves. Like for instance going to church. That got them off the farm (remember their employer was like their dad and they couldn't just wander off without his permission whenever they felt like it) and to a place where they could socialise a little bit with people they didn't spend every minute of every day with. (And night with.) As a matter of fact I have it on good authority that they may have gone to the church not because they were so desperate to hear the sermon, but *so they could go to the coffee and cake event afterwards*. (Gasp!)

Also, the kvöldvaka was fun. Especially if someone told a good story that hadn't been told a hundred times already.

Oh, and they played chess! As a matter of fact, *the* single artefact that led to the founding of the National Museum of Iceland was a chess piece that was discovered buried in the ground. It turned out to be really old. Meaning they played chess for fun even back in the days when they *were* allowed to dance, take saunas, and tell bawdy stories around the long fire without the church freaking out about it.

And last but certainly not least, they played sports. More specifically, they played Iceland's national sport: the *glíma*, a form of wrestling where two guys get dressed up in tights and swimming trunks with straps hanging off them, and then proceed to hang on to each other's hips and dance around until one of the guys trips the other so he falls down. I guess you could call it the sporting version of the Vikivaki, and if you haven't seen what it looks like, I urge you to stop reading, go online, and google it. It will make your day.

44 Going to town

Back in the day when Iceland was an oppressed and miserable Danish colony, our overlords passed a decree that they, and only they, were allowed to do business with us. Meaning that if someone in Iceland was caught trading with anyone but an authorised Danish merchant they were in big, big trouble.

Now, your average Icelander would probably have preferred to flip them the bird and to chew on Iceland moss for the rest of his life rather than have to kowtow to those outrageous commands. But alas, human beings tend to be frail, feeble creatures when they are staring temptation in the face, and the Danes had certain things that the Icelanders really, really wanted. Things like flour, timber (for the poor sods that didn't get direct deliveries from Siberia), sugar, and most tantalising of all, the unholy trinity: coffee, tobacco and liquor.

And so, when those poor, persecuted peasants had something to trade - like, say, woolly hats, fish liver oil or lamb carcasses - they would saddle up their horses, make a little convoy, and head into town to see the merchants.

But oh, those merchants. Those dudes were the schizz, man. They towered so far above the blubbering peasantry of the Colony of Iceland that it's a wonder they didn't have perpetual nosebleeds. And they were not about to haul their asses out of bed on a regular day to open up shop for a convoy of snivelling peasants unless they were bloody well in the mood. And sometimes they were just bloody well not in the mood. And those plebs who all reeked of fish oil ... well they'd just have to wait until the next day. Or the next. Or for such a time as was convenient for the merchants to be in the mood.

So what does a poor snivelling peasant do when he is made to wait around indefinitely to trade his stuff? Well, what any reasonable person would do, of course. He got drunk. Not that he needed the excuse, mind - hitting the sauce was pretty common practice for anyone who went to town. In fact, liquor was so inextricably tied up with those excursions that the smell of it was flippantly referred to as the *kaupstaðalykt*, "town smell" - a moniker that is still used today.

By the time the merchant finally opened up shop, the peasant farmer might just be the teeniest bit irate, and the teeniest bit inebriated. And might just decide to express his dissatisfaction, which would inevitably give the merchant an excuse to hop over the store counter and punch the peasant in the face. This, more often than not, would result in a brawl.

So you see that going to town was balls of fun, too.

That was one scenario. The other common scenario was this: whenever the merchant deigned to open, he would always have a wee bottle behind the counter, and would be happy to dole out shots to his pathetic customers with their measly wares. They would then start chatting about the weather or suchlike, the merchant would pour more liquor, the peasant would imbibe, the merchant would repeat as needed, and eventually the peasant would be blotto. At which time the merchant would promptly take the opportunity to cut a deal that was in every way advantageous to his own person, and in no way advantageous to the poor, blubbering peasant.

It will probably not surprise you that Icelandic peasants hated these merchants with an unbridled passion. And even though it was strictly forbidden, they took to trading, whenever possible, directly with the foreigners whose ships were moored offshore. Which I guess *was* their way of flipping the bird, albeit in a somewhat passive-aggressive manner.

45 Grunge scene

We cannot come to the end of this little collection of essays without mentioning the Icelanders' hygiene back in the day.

First, though, let me state the obvious: bad hygiene was pretty standard anywhere in the world in those days. So it's not like the Icelanders were a special case - pretty much everyone was a filthy mess, at least by our current standards.

However, a somewhat curious thing happened with the Icelanders. When the first settlers arrived, and in the era when Icelanders were an independent people, folks seem to have paid a fair bit of attention to their personal hygiene. They would use the numerous warm pools found throughout the country to bathe in, and even built their homes nearby expressly for that purpose.

But as the nation became more oppressed and subjugated and poor, people seem to have become increasingly apathetic about cleanliness. This was particularly true in the 17th and 18th centuries, when it was almost trendy to be dirty. Either that, or it went hand-in-hand with their low sense of self-worth, which, as it happens, is my own preferred theory.

And I guess you can't blame them. They lived in dirt houses, so there was dirt all around. It was impossible to wash the floor (obviously, since it was made of dirt). Later, as wooden floors became more common, the floor was cleaned about once a year. They would put a bit of water on it, and the caked-on dirt would form a layer of scum which was then scraped off and thrown outside.

Then there were the clothes and bed clothes. People washed their shirts every two weeks or so, but their underclothes far less often. There was one man, for instance, who was known to wash his underclothes once a year, at Christmas. He would then wear them until the summer, at which point he would take them off, turn them inside-out, and wear them that way until it was time for another washing.

Apparently people didn't wear their underwear to bed, so that may have helped slightly, although that meant their bedding was the recipient of the dirt. The

bedding was washed maybe once a year, in the spring. It was washed in, um, *urine*, which was considered to be a very good cleanser on account of the ammonia. The downside was that the smell stayed in for weeks afterwards (which may well be why the washing wasn't done more frequently).

As for personal hygiene ... well, let me just say this. Apparently it was considered auspicious to be as dirty as possible. In fact an idiom existed back then that for some bizarre reason has completely vanished from the lexicon: *Saursæll maður er jafnan aursæll* - "a man that is dirty is often wealthy". Filth, in other words, was associated with "filthy rich". Children were washed every now and again, but adults rarely immersed themselves in water. People would wash their faces when they went to church, albeit rather halfheartedly, but their hands only sometimes. Women, apparently, were more conscientious about this, combing their hair and washing their faces on the weekends, although few did so daily. The favoured substance for washing of the body was not water, but rather everyone's favourite cleanser: urine. Soap for washing hands and face first became common among the elite, and moved down through the social ranks to the peasantry in the latter part of the 19th century.

It goes without saying, of course, that fleas and lice were a common problem back then. They tended to breed in the bedding, along with any number of other creepy-crawlies that made their homes in the hay or brushwood that served as mattresses, and which would remain in the same place, untouched, year after year. Amazingly, the popular belief was that lice came from inside the body, and were therefore impossible to eliminate. Naturally they were a massive scourge, and people frequently had open sores on their bodies from the lice bites and the accompanying itching and scratching. Of course people wanted nothing more than to be free from this pestilence, and various methods of achieving this were devised. This included placing crowberry ling under the sheets, or carrying the bones of a dead person on your body. As far as I know, none of those remedies ever achieved the desired result.

46 Grim reaper

Death.

In our day and age, death has become remote, isolated and distant. It is kept behind closed doors and rarely spoken of. It makes most people profoundly uncomfortable. Next to money, it is probably the biggest taboo of our age.

Back in the Iceland of old, death was everywhere. Consider: from 1750 to 1850, three hundred of every thousand children died before they reached their first birthday. Thirty-two percent died within the first three years of their life, and only fifty-seven percent reached confirmation age, or their fourteenth year.

In other words, only about every other person born reached adulthood.

Those children who did survive soon became acquainted with the grim reaper. It is not unlikely that one or both of their parents died while they were still young. If they had grandparents living at the farm, they probably saw them die. They watched animals being slaughtered, or found that they had perished in bad weather. Often this would be like losing a best friend.

Iceland was, and is, a dangerous place. Even today, with all our modern gadgets for reaching remote places, tracking locations and suchlike, accidents happen frequently. Just imagine what it was like back then. A fog or blizzard might sweep in without warning, and a lone traveller would become hopelessly lost. Sometimes people fell off cliffs or escarpments, or into rivers. Or they simply wandered around aimlessly, trying to find their way home, until they died from hypothermia or starvation.

Then there were the disasters at sea. Those open rowboats in which people fished until the 19th century were completely vulnerable in sudden storms, or even just rough seas. And even if the sea was smooth and conditions relatively good, people could still die. One of the most memorable scenes I have read in any book is in the Icelandic novel *Heaven and Hell*, by Jón Kalmann Stefánsson. A man, rowing out to sea with his crew mates, forgets to bring his sea parka. The omission isn't discovered until the boat is too far from land to row back in time, and he freezes to death before their eyes, with them being unable to help him. Harrowing - and probably all too real in the Iceland of old.

So how did people cope with all this death? One theory is that people's frequent moves - from farm to farm, sometimes as often as once a year - stemmed from the fact that they wanted to escape their feelings of grief. And who can blame them? There was no trauma counselling back then, and people probably had no idea how to even begin working through their emotions. Even if they had, the open expression of bereavement would probably not have been welcome inside the cramped quarters of the baðstofa. Besides, debilitating grief was likely not a luxury in which people could indulge, as it interfered with the business of survival. People had no choice but to shut down emotionally and soldier on. And write things like this, which is taken from an actual journal: "There is frost outside, yet it is calm. My daughter died last night."

47 Grief box

Indeed, it is rare to find anything written about people's responses to grief in the Iceland of old. It is a dark and hidden subject.

There is so little written about it that one might be tempted to think that Icelanders back then didn't feel much of anything. That maybe they had developed a thick skin over the centuries and, like animals, could just let their offspring die without dwelling on it too much, or feeling it too much.

But I have heard one touching story that negates this theory. A home was being dissolved by the authorities after the man of the house had died, similar to what I described earlier. The family was going to be split up, the children sent to different farms. Knowing this, their mother decided to create a box for each of them, into which she put objects to remind them of her, their family, and of home. Things like a lock of hair, a piece of cloth that smelled like home, a letter from her, their mother, and so on. The box wasn't very big because they weren't allowed to take many possessions with them - after all, space in the old turf houses was very limited, and each person could only have so much. She told them that when they felt overcome with grief, or completely alone in the world, they could take their box, go someplace where they were alone, and touch the objects one by one, remembering that they were loved.

48 Death superstitions

There is no greater uncertainty in this life than death, and what happens to us afterwards. It is not surprising, therefore, that superstition abounded in the Iceland of old when it came to dying.

For example, folks believed that if you saw your own ghost, it meant that you were about to die (seems logical). If you tripped in a graveyard, it meant you were about to die. If you and another person thought the same thing, and the other person said what you were thinking before you did, it meant that you were about to die - unless you said the words, "I am not more quick to die than God wants me to be". Then you were OK.

If you did something in a disoriented state, or something that was opposed to your usual conduct, it meant you were about to die. If there was the sound of breaking or snapping in a farmhouse, the master of the house was about to die. If the fire went out at the farm between the fardagar (those few days a year when everyone moved house or changed their place of employment) and Midsummer Night - so between approximately 14 May and 24 June - the mistress of the house would die.

If straws, pieces of string, or bits of paper unintentionally landed in a cross on the floor, or if a light went out without cause, someone was about to die. If a mole was heard chewing on something in the wall, someone would die. If a raven crowed on the roof of a farm where there was a sick individual inside, that person would surely die. And there didn't even need to be a sick person. *Someone would die.*

If someone heard the sound of bells in the distance, or heard a ringing in their ears, a person would die. If someone saw a falling star, they would soon hear of a person dying, and the news would come from the direction of the falling star. If something they ate at a farm made them feel sick, someone at that farm would die (maybe of that same food that made them sick?).

If it rained into a grave at a funeral, it meant that another funeral would soon be held.

If two men died at a farm within a short period of time, a third would surely die before a year had passed from the death of the first (um, maybe of the same ailment?).

If a cat refused to sleep in the bed of a sick person, it meant the person would die, especially if the cat was used to sleeping there before. However, if a cat made a point of sleeping in the bed of a sick person, it meant that the person would get better.

If you saw a light in a church, or heard voices from a church, or saw ghosts in a church, someone would die before too long.

The list goes on. In fact, the sheer length of the list of superstitions speaks volumes about the omnipresence of death. If there were so many signs of dying, then surely dying happened *all the time*.

Above all else, the Icelanders believed in destiny. They believed that a person would - and indeed *would have to* - die if their time had come. The Icelanders even have a word for this: *feigur*, meaning "someone who is about to die and there is nothing that anyone can do about it".

There was a story of a man, for instance, who had planned to ride into a raging river but was forced by his travel companions to turn back because it was too dangerous. Soon afterwards, the man became gravely ill. It was pretty obvious that he wouldn't make it, yet he struggled to give up the ghost. This "death war" (as the Icelanders call it) went on for a long while, and the man was clearly suffering. Finally someone had an idea to fetch water from the river into which the dying man had planned to ride. A few drops were sprinkled on him, and he died almost instantly. Conclusion: it had been his destiny to drown in the river that day, he had been feigur, and since that destiny had been arrested, he could only die by having water from the river sprinkled on him.

49 Last rites

When someone died, they had to sigh three times for it to be considered, well, *valid*. If they did not, that meant that they probably weren't dead, even if they appeared to be.

When that third sigh had passed from the dying person's lips, someone would quickly go to the skjár - you remember, that makeshift window in the roof - and remove it so the soul could escape. When the soul had (presumably) flown into the vast blue yonder, it was time for last rites. The person's eyes and mouth were shut, and also, if possible, the nostrils. The corpse was then laid on its back, and the hands were crossed over the chest. When rigour mortis had set in, the corpse was placed on a plank and wrapped in some kind of shroud. This was then fastened in two or three places, and the whole bundle carried into some other room where it waited to be placed in a coffin, if one was available.

I say "if" because, well, they weren't always available (remember the lack-of-wood dilemma). So peasants were often buried sans coffin - and sometimes even sans plank. This was especially common when there were epidemics, or times were especially hard and lots of people died.

Sometimes there would be no room at the farm to keep a dead body. In such cases it was often taken to the church right away, and leaned up against a wall somewhere. This was considered to be a pretty stellar solution, because not only did it solve the space issue, the holy spirits wafting around the church would prevent evil spirits from entering the corpse and turning it into a zombie.

It was fairly common practice to keep a vigil over the dead body until it had been placed in the coffin (or put on the plank, or whatever). This vigil would usually last for three nights at the farm and three nights in the church. Usually two people kept vigil over the body - normally young women. The light was kept on if it was dark outside, and it was essential that the light did not go out. The corpse did not need to be watched over during the day, but definitely at night.

A body was usually transported to the church on horseback. The coffin or body was then carried through the lychgate while the church bells rang and people sang hymns. There was generally no sermon in the church - only singing. Afterwards the coffin or body would be carried back out of the church and in a circle around it before being placed in the grave. In some places, like the island of Grímsey, the coffin was turned around in three circles after it had been carried out of the church.

If the dead person was an executed criminal, or someone who had committed suicide, burial in a church yard was not allowed. Nor could the body be carried through the lychgate - instead it was lifted over the enclosure surrounding the yard. Neither could such delinquents be buried inside the church yard - their grave had to be outside of it, and preferably some distance away.

Today when someone dies, there is a funeral, and

almost always an *erfidrykkja* afterwards. This is a get-together where the guests meet, talk, and enjoy refreshments. The same was true back in the day, although our *erfidrykkjur* today pale in comparison with those in the past. They could be pretty rambunctious, replete with eating and drinking ... as in, *real* drinking, and plenty of it. Though to be fair, such feasts were usually only held if the deceased person was someone of means.

In the late 19th century, something called *húskveðjur* - "house farewells" - became common. Guests would arrive at the home of the deceased early in the day, eat something, and then bid farewell to the deceased person, who lay in an open casket. Afterward the entire congregation would head to the church for the burial, and then return to the house, where rice pudding and some kind of meat dish would be offered, followed by coffee. Occasionally there might be alcohol served, though nothing in comparison to the erfidrykkjur of earlier times.

The húskveðjur were abolished in the mid-20th century after a "grave tax" was levied on all burials. Its purpose was to fund the construction of a new cemetery, mortuary and chapel. The idea behind it was that the húskveðjur would no longer need to be held in people's homes, but rather could be held in the chapel. And this is exactly what happened - húskveðjur were abolished in the early 1960s, but exist today in the form of *kistulagningar*. The *kistulagning* is essentially an open casket ceremony, held a couple of days (or sometimes a couple of hours) before the funeral proper. Those closest to the deceased then come together and say their goodbyes

privately. This helps to remove the sting of grief, allow-
ing people to release their deepest feelings among their
closest friends and relatives before having to face the
funeral guests, which typically can number upwards of
a hundred people. Today, you see, we Icelanders enjoy
a luxury that our forebears did not - we get to honour
our grief, and give it the space it needs.

50 The role of hope

I mentioned earlier that it was a wonder how people
managed to survive, emotionally and physically, with
all the hardship and grief in the Iceland of old. What
kept them going? Why didn't they just … check out?

Well, one theory is that they *did* check out - or at least
some of them did. Those who couldn't take it simply
died off, while the more robust among them carried on
- the classic tale about the survival of the fittest. In that
way, hardy resiliance became bred into the constitution
of the Icelandic people.

But even so, there was one single ingredient that people *had to have* if they wanted to keep on living. They
had to have hope. Hope that things would eventually
get better, that they would see brighter days. Yet …
where to find it when there was so much death, grief,
adversity and oppression all around?

We have already discussed the importance of stories.

For the Icelanders of old, stories were an anti-depressant. That is why people clung to them, and by extension to the literary tradition. The Icelanders looked to those stories, internalised them, told them again and again, *lived* them. The stories provided hope.

Faith in God was another factor. The perpetual message from ecclesiastical authorities was that if you believed in God, feared God, avoided temptation and took the high moral ground, things would turn out all right. Besides, if all else failed and adversity did prevail, you could always blame God. If your daughter died young, it was because "God called her". If all your livestock died it was "God's will". There was a reason. It wasn't just senseless or arbitrary.

Also, people learned a certain humility from living with such a landscape and climate. How could they not? There was no bargaining with the landscape; people had no illusions of conquering it. They learned to submit to something greater and far more powerful than themselves. That submission is what humility is all about. And that, of course, is far more conducive to survival than any arrogance or illusion of power. Today we can defer learning those lessons in a number of ways, though eventually life brings all of us to our knees. Back in the Iceland of old, people were brought to their knees pretty much as soon as they could walk.

The past of a nation is always inextricably tied up with its present. All its experiences become a part of its collective identity and soul. Today, Icelanders consistently rank among the happiest people on earth. In survey after survey they claim to be generally optimistic and content with their lot. Why? Why are people who live on a remote island far up in the North Atlantic ocean, who moreover have very little daylight for several months of the year, happier than, say, a person living in sun-kissed Spain or delightful Italy? Could it be that this contentment, this optimism, became ingrained into the very soul of the Icelandic people through centuries of harsh living, when they had to have hope to survive, even when it was completely illogical?

I like to think so. Just as I like to think that Iceland's powerful literary tradition stems from the kvöldvaka, or that the Icelanders' issues with commitment stem from living with a capricious climate. One could draw any number of parallels between the present and the past. Yet I have no definitive answers, and I doubt anyone does.

IN CLOSING

I hope you have enjoyed this little gander at the psychology and history of the Icelandic people. If you have, please consider giving this book a review on Amazon, Goodreads, or wherever you share your love of books. This is an independently published project, and all help getting the word out is hugely appreciated. I also hope that you will join me on facebook.com/icelandweatherreport, or twitter.com/aldakalda, for more fun and no-so-fun facts about Iceland and the Icelanders.

Thanks for reading.

ACKNOWLEDGEMENTS

I am deeply indebted to some people for their help with this project.

To Christopher Condit, Clara Cunha, Ingvar Gíslason, Sylvia Hikins and Sarah Larsen, for reading over the manuscript and offering invaluable critiques and pointers.

To Megan Herbert, for being such a pleasure to work with.

And especially to my husband, Erlingur Páll Ingvarsson, for designing the book and caring about it with me. To say nothing of all the pep talks he routinely gives me, and his endless moral support.

A VERY SPECIAL THANK YOU ...

To all the people who helped out by supporting this project on Indiegogo. This is an independently produced effort, and a fundraising campaign was launched to help offset the cost of production. These people chipped in with extremely generous donations, and have my unending thanks, for their financial contribution as well as for their encouragement and faith in me.

Donald Richmond
Trudy Ditton
Rev. Stefan M. Jonasson
Sally Herbert
Pierre L'Allier
Katharine Wiley
Sunna Furstenau
Julia Malik

ABOUT THE AUTHOR

Alda Sigmundsdóttir is a writer, journalist, translator and blogger. She is the author of three other books: *Unraveled – a Novel About a Meltdown*, *The Little Book of the Icelanders*, and *Living Inside the Meltdown*. In addition, Alda has published a book of Icelandic folk tales in English translation, entitled *Icelandic Folk Legends – Tales of Apparitions, Outlaws and Things Unseen*. She has also written extensively about Iceland for the international media. Alda currently lives in Reykjavík.

SOURCES

These are the most notable sources I used in the writing of this book:

Ágústsson, Hörður. "Íslenski torfbærinn." ["The Icelandic Turf Farm."] Íslensk þjóðmenning, 1 (1987): 227-344. Print.

Björnsson, Árni. *Merkisdagar á mannsævinni*. [*Landmarks of a Lifetime*.] 2nd ed. Reykjavík: Mál Og Menning, 1996. 13-42. Print.

Gunnlaugsson, Gísli Ágúst. "Um fjölskyldusögurannsóknir og íslensku fjölskylduna 1801-1930." ["On Family History Research and the Icelandic Family 1801-1930."] Saga (1986): 7-43. Print.

Hálfdánarson, Guðmundur. "Börn, höfuðstóll fátæklingsins." ["Children, the Pauper's Capital."] Saga (1986): 121-46. Print.

Jónasson, Jónas, and Einar Ól. Sveinsson. *Íslenzkir þjóðhættir* [*Icelandic Folkways*]. 4th ed. Reykjavík: Opna, 2010. Print.

Ólafsson, Guðmundur. "Ljósfæri og lýsing." ["Light Sources and Lighting."] Íslensk þjóðmenning, 1 (1987): 345-69. Print.

Þorsteinsson, Guðmundur. *Horfnir starfshættir og leiftur frá liðnum öldum.* [*Lost Working Methods and Flashes from Centuries Past.*] Reykjavík: Örn og Örlygur, 1990. Print.

"Ættarvefur Hans Jónatans." ["Hans Jónatan's Family Website."] *Ættarvefur Hans Jónatans*. N.p., n.d. Web.

I am also indebted to Eirikur Valdimarsson and Sigurður Gylfi Magnússon who taught the course "Lice Combs, Chamber Pots and Sex: Customs, Traditions and Daily Life in the Rural Society of Iceland" in the spring term of 2012 at the University of Iceland, which truly opened my eyes to the fascinating ways of the Icelanders in the old days.

LITTLE BOOK OF THE ICELANDERS IN THE OLD DAYS
© Alda Sigmundsdóttir, 2014

Enska textasmidjan
Reykjavík, 2014

Illustrations: Megan Herbert
Layout and cover design: Erlingur Páll Ingvarsson
Printing: Prentmidlun Ltd., Poland

ISBN 978-9935-9177-7-5

ENSKA TEXTASMIÐJAN